The Musical Dream Tarot

Praise for The Musical Dream Tarot ...

In *The Musical Dream Tarot*, Dr. Hoffman demonstrates a vast amount of knowledge of hidden information, archaeological knowledge, and esoteric truths, adding to his prodigious and creative dreaming of musical annotations for Tarot. His systematic way of organizing the musical Tarot comes from his frequent, detailed dreams that are riveting as creative compositions in new music. Dr. Hoffman's dream process has organized and constructed a singular set of archeological, astrological, and spiritual correspondences that hang together esoterically, musically, methodologically, and in the sublime order of the psyche of dreaming.

This is a rollicking, page-turning academic read of the mysteries of Tarot and dream music unveiled, a skillful combination of subjective dream interpretation, Tarot knowledge, and esoteric correspondences. It connects the Tarot Keys, the traditional musical keys, and planetary-astrological music traditions: a new qualitative methodology taps into the psyche… worthy of teaching to graduate students in traditional and transpersonal levels of psychology. The vessel that is Curt becomes a suitable channel for a source, mystical, or spiritual presence larger than himself. His accomplishments academically and esoterically have prepared him for the reception of this voluminous creative work as revelatory of the spiritual path of Tarot, dreams, and music.

> —Dr. Ava Lindberg, Ph.D., Jungian depth psychologist, cultural anthropologist, Adjunct professor, advanced research methods, MACP, Sofia University, Palo Alto, CA

~~~~~~~~~~~~~~~~~~~~

The Musical Dream Tarot is one of the most amazing creations I have ever come across, music of a somewhat Renaissance yet celestial nature originating spontaneously within the author's dreams, masterfully composed, inspired and aligned with the essence of each Tarot card. In this book the author leads you through his synchronistically interwoven mystical journey of creation – led by a consistent "we will show you" instruction and encouragement from within the dreams themselves. It provides the reader with a highly researched journey through the ancient origins of the Tarot and music itself while leaving you in awe of the unbounded depths and creativity of dreaming.

> — Bob Hoss, Past President of the International Association for the Study of Dreams and Director of the DreamScience Foundation

The Musical Dream Tarot provides an innovative means for tapping into the archetypes. One is able to appreciate the compositions without having to be a musician. As a Tarot instructor I have added Curtiss' masterpiece to my syllabus. Typically, I advise my students to meditate upon each card at bedtime in order to incubate dreams to further and more directly illuminate the Wisdom of the Tarot; having accompanying music to aid in deeper communion is an invaluable resource to bring the student in resonance with each of the Tarot Keys and the four suits.

Curtiss' suggestion to use the music and Tarot imagery on his website for potential healing is a refreshing perspective on a historic system as the use of sound as a healing tool dates back thousands of years. His motivation in creating this project, to be of service, strikes a chord in me being a student of the Arcane School who seeks "to serve and not exact due service."

—Maria Carla Cernuto, Esoteric Teacher and Tarot Reader

~~~~~~~~~~~~~~~~~~~~~~~

Curtiss Hoffman's book, *The Musical Dream Tarot*, is a profound work of scholarship and inspiration. Dr. Hoffman elucidates how he received music in dreams to accompany the Major and Minor Arcana of the Tarot. The work is stunning in its profound depth and intricacy... a lifetime of study and encyclopedic knowledge of classical music, dreamwork, anthropology, esoterica, and Kabbalah has been brought together to enhance the understanding and mystical experience of Tarot images and their potency to expand consciousness. I was inspired and so impressed reading the manuscript, and learned much about Tarot. I am excited to practice more with contemplating the images while listening to their corresponding music. Highly recommended!

—Lauren Z. Schneider, MA, MFT, Institute of Dreams and Tarotpy®

Music will be largely employed in construction, and in one hundred years from now it will be a feature in certain work of a constructive nature. This sounds to you utterly impossible, but it will simply be the utilization of ordered sound to achieve certain ends.

—Alice A. Bailey, Letters on Occult Meditation. Lucis Publishing, New York, 1922. p. 250

The Musical Dream Tarot

Curtiss Hoffman

The Musical Dream Tarot
Copyright © 2024 Curtiss Hoffman

All rights reserved. No part of this book may be reproduced without the written prior permission of the author.

ISBN: 978-1-952194-30-6

Cover image: **Judgement**, Major Arcana no. 20, from *Pholarcos Tarot* deck used by permission of the artist, Carmen Sorrenti https://www.carmensorrenti.com

Back cover decorative element courtesy of Victorian Free Vector Pack http://www.vectorian.net/download-free-vector-ornaments.html

Printed in the United States of America

RIVER SANCTUARY PUBLISHING
P.O Box 1561
Felton, CA 95018
www.riversanctuarypublishing.com
Dedicated to the awakening of the New Earth

Table of Contents

List of Figures i

Acknowledgements iii

1 — The Tarot – An Introduction 1

2 — Music and Dreams 6

3 — The Gilgamesh Cantata 13

4 — The Origins of the Project 18

5 — The Matrix 23

6 — Methodology 34

7 — Results of the Project 45

8 — The Major Arcana 55

9 — The Minor Arcana – Wands 80

10 — The Minor Arcana – Cups 89

11 — The Minor Arcana – Swords 99

12 — The Minor Arcana – Pentacles 109

13 — How to Access and Use the Music Files 118

Bibliography 121

About the Author 127

List of Figures

1.1:	The Qabbalistic Tree of Life	2
3.1:	Gilgamesh Cantata Dream Types	16
3.2:	Pre-Completion Gilgamesh Cantata Dream Types	16
4.1:	Tarot Cards Drawn in Answer to My Question	18
4.2:	Monthly Tabulation of Tarot and Non-Tarot Dreams	20
4.3:	Percentage of Nights Containing Tarot Dreams, by Month	21
4.4:	Eb Tune #6	22
4.5:	Segment of the Score for the Four of Cups	22
5.1:	Assignment of Major Arcana to Musical keys	26
5.2:	Instruments Used for Musical Dream Tarot Keys	27
5.3:	Musical Keys in Tarot Dreams	28
5.4:	Musical keys Assigned to Major and Minor Arcana Keys	32
5.5:	Time Signatures Associated with Tarot Tunes	33
6.1:	Dream Reentries with Musical Dream Tarot Themes	34
6.2:	Duplicate Tarot Tunes	35
6.3:	Musical Dream Tarot Dreams per Month Attributed to Major and Minor Arcana	38
6.4:	Musical Dream Tarot Dreams by Month by Type of Dream	39
6.5:	Sample Month's Dreaming by Position of the Tarot Dream in the Night	39
6.6:	Sample of Minor Arcana Themes Arranged by Musical Key and Tarot Key	40
6.7:	Sample of Major Arcana Themes Arranged by Musical Key and Tarot Key	40
6.8:	Number of Measures for Dream Tunes	41
6.9:	Final Attribution of Dreams to Sword Keys, and Timing of the Pieces	43
7.1:	Frequencies of Major and Minor Arcana Dreams by Month	45
7.2:	Distribution of Musical Dream Tarot Dreams by Type of Dream	47
7.3:	Number of Nights with Only One Recalled Dream, by Month	48
7.4:	Number of Nights with 2, 3, 4, or 5 Recalled Dreams, by Month	48
7.5:	Average Position of Tarot Dreams within the Night's Dreaming	49
7.6:	Word Count Averages for Musical Dream Tarot Dream Types	50
7.7:	Average Word Counts by Dream Position for Dream Types	51
7.8:	Average Word Count by Position for All Tarot Dreams	51
7.9:	Average Word Count by Dream Type for First, Middle, and Last Tarot Dreams	52

Acknowledgements

First, I wish to acknowledge Mr. Anthony Bonello, who (as described in Chapter 2) introduced me to the Tarot during my twenties and who gave me valuable instruction on how to interpret its symbols. Next, I want to credit Lauren Schneider and Carmen Sorrenti, whose dedication to the Tarot and its symbols reawakened my own interest and sparked this project. Thanks go to my wife, Tobi, my sons Darrel and Adam, and my granddaughter Violet, upon all of whom I inflicted early versions of the music. My faculty colleague Mike Zimmerman assisted me in setting up the website which accompanies this book. I also wish to thank Dr. Donald Running, the director of the Bridgewater State University Wind Ensemble, who encouraged me in this project and who provided opportunities for five members of the ensemble to try out some of the pieces in rehearsal and, eventually, performance. The Bridgewater State University Retired Faculty Club supported me with a small grant which enabled me to provide the performing students in the Wind Ensemble with a stipend for their work on performing some of the pieces. Finally, thanks go to my publisher, Annie Elizabeth Porter of River Sanctuary Publishing, whose enthusiasm for this project lifted it into the realm of manifestation, and to Bill Gorman, who provided the essential connection to River Sanctuary.

◆ 1 ◆
The Tarot – An Introduction

This book describes a major creative project which I undertook from June of 2021 through January of 2023, to create music provided by my dreams to accompany the cards of the Tarot deck. For those who are unfamiliar with the Tarot, it is a deck of 78 cards (called "Keys") bearing archetypal images. The first 22 of these Keys, titled and numbered from 0 to 21, are considered the "Major Arcana", and they incorporate deep archetypes and complex symbolic imagery. The remaining 56 cards, the "Minor Arcana", are divided into four suits (traditionally called Wands, Swords, Cups, and Pentacles) of 14 cards each, numbered from Ace to 10 followed by four court cards: Kings, Queens, Knights, and Pages. These suits are the origin of the Clubs, Spades, Hearts, and Diamonds (respectively) of the familiar playing card deck. The imagery of these cards tends to be less complex than that of the Major Arcana.

The origins of the Tarot are, to say the least, obscure. Some 18th - 19th century occultists tried to link the images to the writings of the Neoplatonist philosopher Iamblichus, who claimed to have been initiated in an Egyptian temple to the god Serapis in the vicinity of modern Naples in the 3rd century, A.D.[1] This temple was purported to display the images of twenty of the Major Arcana in succession, representing the stages of the initiatory process, while the god was represented by one of the two remaining images and the initiand by the other. However, the evidence for the existence of these images in the temple – which was destroyed by bombing during World War II – is very scanty and conjectural.[2]

Another important source, though not initially related to the visual images, is the Qabbalah, a source of Jewish mysticism which has its documented origins in the same period as Iamblichus, but which was much elaborated during the Middle Ages by Diaspora Jews in Spain and southern France. One of the most important early texts for the Qabbalah is the *Sefer Yetzirah*, the Book of Formation, whose origins are unknown but which has 2nd century, A.D. commentaries by authentic rabbinical sources.[3] It documents thirty-two paths of wisdom, the first ten of which are the spheres (Sephiroth) associated with the Earth, the visible planets, the sphere of the zodiac, and that of the Creator, the Prime Mover (*Primum Mobile*). The remaining 22 are

---

[1] Thomas Taylor, *Iamblichus on the Mysteries of the Egyptians, Chaldeans, and Assyrians*. Forgotten Books, London UK, 2018.
[2] Charles King, *The Gnostics and Their Remains*. http://www.luxlapis.co.za/at/serapis.htm.
[3] Aryeh Kaplan, trans. *Sefer Yetzirah: The Book of Creation*. Weiser Books, New York, 1997.

paths connecting the Sephiroth which correspond to the 22 letters of the Hebrew alphabet, as shown in Figure 1.1[4]. These paths were later associated with the 22 Major Arcana of the Tarot.

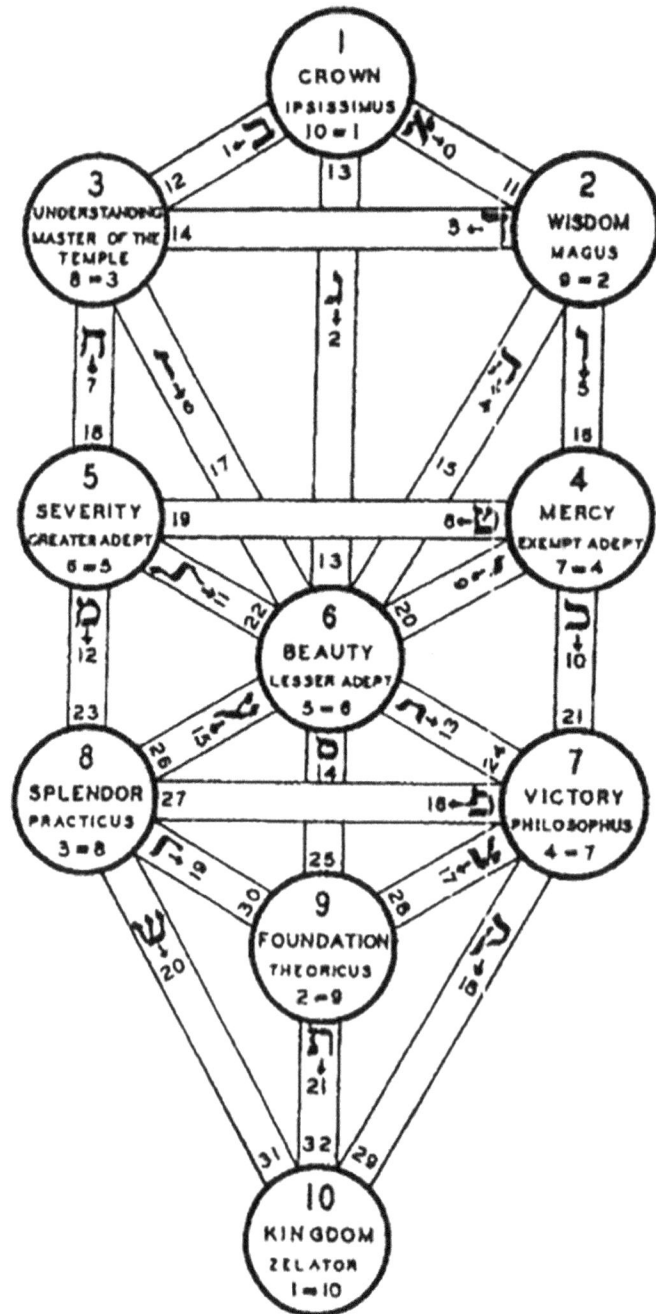

Figure 1.1 The Qabbalistic Tree of Life

---

[4] Paul Foster Case, *The Tarot: A Key to the Wisdom of the Ages*. Macoy Publishing Company, Richmond VA, 1947. p. 224. The number of each associated Tarot Key may be derived from the figure by subtracting 11 from the number on its path in Figure 1.1 (e.g., Path 11 = Key 0).

There are also accounts of the origin of the Tarot being the result of an international conclave of scholars meeting in the Moroccan city of Fez (modern Fas) around 1200 A.D., at a time of somewhat relaxed tolerance among Christians, Muslims, and Jews in the western Mediterranean area.[5] However, evidence for the existence of this conclave is also conjectural.

At least by the late 14th century A.D., however, there is clear evidence that the deck, or portions of it, was in popular use throughout Western Europe, in the form of playing cards called "Tarocchi," an Italian word meaning foolishness.[6] Some scholars consider that these cards originated in northern Italy, and that gambling was the original purpose for which they were devised.[7] While the earliest known examples were hand-painted, they were more widely disseminated with the advent of the printing press. However, most playing card decks lack the Major Arcana (except for the Fool, which became the Joker) and eliminate one of the court cards (either the Knight or the Page, depending upon how the Jack or Knave is interpreted). The depicted Tarocchi images, and their ordering, were somewhat variable in this period.

Despite this somewhat materialist interpretation of its origins, the system of images which the Major Arcana of the Tarot presented up until the late 20th Century is highly consistent and is tightly interwoven with other symbol systems current in Renaissance Europe, including astrology, the Hebrew alphabet, geometry, alchemy, anatomical symbolism, etc.[8] – as I will show in Chapter Eight. For this reason, I find it difficult to believe that it was originally intended principally for the purpose of gambling. A more likely scenario, in my opinion, is that the images were originally devised as meditation seeds, but because Catholic Church authorities disfavored this use (as it was felt to be an expression of paganism), the cards drifted to the margins of the European societies of the time (e.g. the Roma) in the form of fortune-telling cards, and eventually these were transformed into the familiar gambling cards[9]. The context of their initial widespread popularity may very well have been linked to the rekindling of interest in the belief systems of the classical world which characterized the Renaissance, especially in northern Italy. In my estimation, the Minor Arcana, with the exception of the court cards and Aces, convey a much less consistent system. Each of

---

[5] Ibid, p.2.
[6] Patti Wigington, A Brief History of Tarot. https://www.learnreligions.com/a-brief-history-of-tarot-2562770, 2018.
[7] Kelly Richman-Abdou, *The Spellbinding History of Tarot Cards, from a Mainstream Card Game to a Magical Ritual.* https://mymodernmet.com/history-of-tarot-cards/
[8] Hardin Craig, ed., *The Complete Works of Shakespeare.* Scott, Foresman, and Company, Chicago IL,1951, p.10..
[9] This view is supported by Christine Payne-Towler, The Esoteric Origins of Tarot. https://www.tarot.com/tarot/christine-payne-towler/esoteric-origins. The new wealth flowing into the Italian trade cities at that time would have provided the means for members of the moneyed classes to indulge in gambling.

the numbered cards, to be sure, has the requisite number of elemental symbols, but beyond that their symbolism seems, at least to me, to be somewhat arbitrary and less archetypal. This may be the reason that the images were eventually dropped from the gambling cards, as well as from Paul Foster Case's Tarot deck[10]. Thinking now as an archaeologist accustomed to seeing the evolution of material culture over time, I suggest that it is possible that the northern Italian Tarocchi were originally just the 56 Minor Arcana (or some subset of them[11]), used for gambling, onto which the older Major Arcana images were grafted in the late 14th century. This could resolve the apparent conflict between the two perspectives described above.

P.D. Ouspensky, in his magisterial *A New Model of the Universe*[12], describes the Tarot as a "kind of philosophical abacus" and defines its purpose as follows:

a) It gives a possibility of setting out in different graphic forms . . . ideas which are difficult if not impossible to put into words.

b) It is an instrument of the mind, an instrument which can serve for training the capacity for combination and so on.

c) It is an appliance for exercising the mind, for accustoming it to new and wider concepts, to thinking in a world of higher dimensions, and to the understanding of symbols.

The emergence, or reemergence, of the Western esoteric tradition in the 18th and 19th centuries resulted in a massive revival of interest among the literati of that time in the Tarot as a system of symbols, and many individual esotericists and occult groups adopted it as a means of communicating arcane wisdom to their acolytes.[13] This resulted in some standardization of both the imagery and the order of the Major Arcana in particular. The best-known of the Tarot decks, authorized by Arthur Edward Waite and painted by Pamela Coleman Smith, dates to 1909[14], and is still widely used today.

The emergence of the New Age movement, starting in the late 1960s and continuing to the present, has resulted in a veritable explosion of variations on the traditional 78-card deck. Many of these new decks retain the structure of the Rider-Waite deck, but with more artistically drawn images. I am particularly fond of the images of the Major Arcana drawn by Jessie Burns Parke

---

[10] Case, op. cit., passim.

[11] Suzanna Stanska, The Mystery of the Mantegna Tarocchi. *DailyArt Magazine.* https://www.dailyartmagazine.com/mystery-mantegna-tarocchi/, 2022.

[12] P.D. Ouspensky, *A New Model of the Universe.* Borzoi Books, New York, 1931. pp. 188-189. It should be noted that Ousepensky's ordering of the Major Arcana is highly idiosyncractic!

[13] Wigington, op. cit.

[14] Arthur Edward Waite, *The Rider Tarot Deck.* U.S. Games Systems, Inc., Stamford CT, 2019.

at the direction of Paul Foster Case[15] and promulgated by the Builders of the Adytum organization which he founded[16]. Some of the newer decks incorporate imagery taken from a variety of alternative cultures, such as Japanese, ancient Egyptian, Native American, and Wiccan. Strephon Kaplan-Williams' Dream Cards[17] abandon the 78-card format and offer 66 archetypal images, not arranged by suits. Some other decks use the 64 hexagrams of the *I Ching* as the basis for their cards[18].

The principal purpose of the images in all of these variations, as in the more traditional Tarot decks, is to draw forth a deep intuitive response from the viewer, whether this be a person seeking a Tarot reading for advice from an experienced reader, or someone meditating upon the images for self-development. In this sense, all of these decks "work", in the sense that they are capable of evoking a psychological response in the viewer. However, numerous practitioners report that something much more powerful is often going on during a "reading". Remarkable coincidences and synchronicities[19] are often observed between the cards drawn and issues current in the querent's life. There seems to be a fundamental wisdom operating behind the scenes here; it seems as if SOMEONE knows what they are about and that the selection of cards, though seemingly random, actually provides surprisingly intelligible and poignantly accurate answers. It was certainly in the spirit of acceptance of an unseen source of guidance that I undertook the current project.

---

[15] Case, op. cit., p.20.
[16] Case, op. cit., p,14.
[17] Strephon Kaplan-Williams, *Dream Cards: Understand Your Dreams and Enrich Your Life*. Fireside, Gleneden Beach, OR, 1991.
[18] e.g., I Ching Holitzka Deck. U.S. Games Systems, Inc., Stamford CT, 1999.
[19] C.G. Jung and Wolfgang Pauli, Synchronicity: An Acasual Connecting Principle. In *The Structure and Dynamics of the Psyche. Collected Works* v. 8, trans R.F.C. Hull. Princeton University Press, Princeton NJ, 1970.

◆ 2 ◆
Music and Dreams

I next wish to provide some background on my musical pedigree. My maternal grandfather was a violinist and violin-maker who emigrated to the U.S. from Romania. I was exposed to classical music at an early age. I can recall myself as a boy of 8 or so dancing alone in my basement to the sounds of Enescu's First Romanian Rhapsody. As a result, I developed a lifelong passion for Western classical music. I played clarinet from the age of 10 until the end of my junior year in college. In my house, the radio is almost always tuned to a local classical music station, so music is around me all the time. I did a little composing as a high school student, some of which was actually performed at a public concert during my senior year. But I put that part of my skill set aside for many years, as I pursued a professional career in archaeology.

During my college and graduate school years, I amassed a very large collection of classical LP records, and I became increasingly familiar with the canons of Western classical music, at least from the Baroque period onwards. This familiarity allows me easily to recognize many musical compositions from only a few notes. This skill would prove useful in deciding which dream tunes to include within or to exclude from the Musical Dream Tarot, as it enabled me quickly to identify previously written compositions which appeared in my dreams. My taste ran (and still runs) most strongly to the late 19th and early 20th century Romantic composers.

I also developed an interest in dreams and in world mythology in my teen years, in part sparked by a TV series on the local PBS channel hosted by Joseph Campbell on depth psychology[1]. I was more strongly drawn to Jung than to Freud, and I read many of the volumes of Jung's *Collected Works*[2] during my college and graduate school years. My interest in symbolism led me to create my own complex, interlocking symbol system with its own language, calendar, and mythology. I brought friends whom I found receptive to it into this system; in effect, it was a little polytheistic religious cult of its own.

In the winter of 1969, during my first year of graduate school at Yale University in New Haven, Connecticut, one of those friends introduced me to a spiritual teacher, whose outer name was Anthony Bonello, but who had an esoteric designation as Master 7 8. He offered a powerful mix of Eastern Hindu and Buddhist yoga teachings and Western esoteric traditions, including

---

[1] Joseph Campbell, Audio Lectures, Series One, pre-1970. https://jcf.org/lectures/.
[2] Carl Gustav Jung, *Collected Works*. 20 volumes. *Bollingen Series* XX, Princeton University Press, Princeton NJ. 1957-1977.

Qabbalah and astrology, as well as the books of Alice A. Bailey, published by the Arcane School.[3] These books were transmitted to Bailey telepathically by a Tibetan teacher, Djwahl Khul, who then edited the received manuscripts which she sent to him by mail.[4] I attended a group ritual Master 7 8 conducted in Boston, based upon the Qabbalistic Tree of Life. Afterwards, two of his senior disciples informed me that they were driving his wife back to New York City where he lived, while he remained in Boston to teach his other disciples. They offered me a ride back to New Haven. This happened to be the night of the great Northeast blizzard of 1969, and it took us more than five hours to get to New Haven, a trip which ordinarily would have taken two. All the way there, we conversed about the correspondences between the symbol system I had "independently" devised and the symbol system used by the group – and we found that they fit together very closely. It was on this basis that I decided to join Master 7 8's group of students, The Servers of the Great Ones (SOTGO).

While our teacher never fully explained the meaning of 7 8 to his group, I have found a number of striking synchronicities, as Jung called them,[5] with this pair of numbers. First, of course, there are 78 cards in the Tarot deck, and the study of Tarot was one of the areas to which he introduced us. This was, in fact, my first exposure to the cards and their symbolism. In addition, it turned out that Master 7 8 lived precisely 7.8 miles from my parents' house; that one of the pieces of music which had most strongly moved me in my undergraduate years, the Saint-Saens Organ Symphony, is that composer's Opus 78; and that Immanuel Velikovsky, an unorthodox researcher who was my early mentor[6], and with whom I corresponded during my later high school and early college years, lived at an address in Princeton, New Jersey (where Jung's books were published in English translation) whose street number was 78.

Master 7 8 also asked us to keep a journal of spiritual impressions, including those related to the Tarot. Reviewing this journal in the hindsight of about 50 years, I was surprised to find numerous gems of insight, some of which I have incorporated into my descriptions of the Major Arcana in Chapter Eight. Some of these are poetical statements placed in quotes, and are intuitions received during my meditations on the Keys. At a certain point in our training, each of us was asked to select two of the Major Arcana with which we most strongly resonated, and, taking the sum of their numbers, to construct for ourselves a ritual name, using the number values of the letters

---

[3] Alice A. Bailey, *24 Books of Esoteric Philosophy.* Lucis Publishing, New York, 1919-1949.
[4] Alice A. Bailey, *The Unfinished Autobiography.* Lucis Publishing, New York, 1951. pp.258-261.
[5] Carl Gustav Jung and Wolfgang Pauli, Synchronicity: An Acausal Connecting Principle. *Collected Works* v.8, *The Structure and Dynamics of the Psyche. BollingenSeries* XX. Princeton University Press, Princeton NJ, 1970.
[6] Immanuel Velikovsky, *Worlds in Collision.* Macmillan, New York, 1950.

of the Hebrew alphabet – another of the subjects we studied.[7] In the Qabbalistic treatise *The Zohar*[8], written around the same time as the possible origins of the Tarot in the 12th century, each of these letters is associated with a particular mode of consciousness, and each of them forms one of the 22 paths on the Tree of Life diagram[9]. The cards I chose were Key 16, The Tower, and Key 6, The Lovers. Their sum, 22, provided me with the name Chabib ("Beloved"), which has the same numerical value by the above system.[10]

I spent seven charmed years at the feet of Master 7 8, essentially all the rest of my graduate school training and beyond. Without a doubt, his teachings influenced my choice of a doctoral dissertation topic. I worked on the animal symbolism found on the cylindrical stone seals used by the ancient Mesopotamians to authenticate their identity on documents. I was able to show that these designs were part of a complex symbol system which was related to their astrological system[11], which was the basis for all subsequent astrological systems throughout the Mediterranean basin and which is still used by modern astrologers[12]. I was able to reduce the complexity of the animal motifs on the seals to only four ethnozoographic categories: carnivores, oviparous animals (including arthropods, fish, reptiles, and birds), humans, and herbivores. The title of the dissertation referred to the most common representative members of these four categories: *The Lion, the Eagle, the Man, and the Bull in Mesopotamian Glyptic*[13]. The heads of these four animals often appear at the corners of Tarot Keys 10 (The Wheel of Fortune) and 21 (The World), and they also represent the astrological signs of Leo, Scorpio, Aquarius, and Taurus, respectively – these four signs marked the stations of the sunrise on the solstices and equinoxes at the time (ca. 3,000 B.C.) when the system was devised. They also are mentioned in the visionary experiences of Ezekiel in the Old Testament[14] and of John in the New Testament[15] as the "Four Living Creatures", the conveyors of the Chariot of God.

---

[7] In this system, the first 10 letters, starting with Aleph, represent the numbers from 1 to 10; the next nine represent the numbers 20 through 100, counting by tens, and the last three letters represent the numbers 200 through 400, counting by hundreds.

[8] Daniel C. Matt, trans., *The Zohar*. Stanford University Press, Palo Alto CA, 2003.

[9] See Figure 1.1, supra.

[10] These names were later superseded by other ritual names, so I feel free to share mine.

[11] Not that a seal represented its owner's birth chart, but rather that the same repertoire of animal symbols projected by the Mesopotamians onto the heavens was also the basis of the seal designs.

[12] All but two of the twelve current zodiacal signs are of Mesopotamian origin. The exceptions are Aries, for which the Mesopotamian equivalent is the plowman, and Cancer, for which the Mesopotamian equivalent is the turtle.

[13] Curtiss Hoffman, *The Lion, the Eagle, the Man, and the Bull in Mesopotamian Glyptic*. University Microfilms, Ann Arbor MI, 1974.

[14] Ezekiel 1:4-28.

[15] Revelations 5:6-9.

After our teacher passed out of incarnation in 1976, the group rapidly degenerated into a tumultuous field of contending egos, and eventually my wife and I left it. However, by this time I had my doctoral degree and I was able to secure a teaching position in Anthropology at Bridgewater State College (now University) in Massachusetts. After an initial trial semester, I was hired in 1978 as a full-time Anthropology faculty member, and I remained in that position until my semi-retirement in 2018. In addition to teaching archaeology courses, I developed new courses in mythology and in culture and consciousness. I continue to teach one course a semester at the university to this day. I continued along the same lines of spiritual exploration as I had followed in SOTGO, and this led me to one of the major areas of influence included in Master 7 8's teachings, the Arcane School. This organization, founded by Alice Bailey in 1923, offers spiritual training through correspondence[16], and I remain an active member of it, attending annual conferences (both in person and, during the COVID pandemic, on-line), webinars, and eventually serving as a "secretary" to assist newer members of the organization.

I began systematically recording my dreams starting in 1992, following a meeting at the Arcane School's annual conference with two other advanced esoteric students, Joy Gates and Gudrun Weber. At the same conference the year before that, the three of us had met for the first time and established a strong affinity. We had agreed to meet in New York a few days before the 1992 conference. Prior to that meeting, each of us had had a very powerful dream, and when we shared them with each other, we discovered that themes from the three dreams wove in and around one another. We realized that we had something very valuable here, and we resolved to send each other thereafter monthly dream reports of all of our remembered dreams. To do this, I used a dream recording database program written for me in Access© by my wife, which allows for the rapid retrieval of keywords of several different categories. This has been invaluable in collecting information on the dreams I used for this project. We continued this practice of dream sharing for at least a dozen years, and the act of recording dreams dramatically increased my dream recall rate, to a point where I was regularly averaging about 45 recalled dreams per month, occasionally with as many as seven dreams on some nights. This frequency is considered to be unusually high by dream researchers[17].

This close friendship led me to the International Association for the Study of Dreams (IASD), an eclectic organization which fosters the investigation of dreams from a wide range of disciplines: from their scientific study in sleep laboratories to the work of neo-shamans and indigenous

---

[16] The Arcane School. https://online.arcaneschool.org/.
[17] e.g. Tore Nielsen, Variations in Dream Recall Frequency and Dream Theme Diversity by Age and Sex. *Frontiers in Neurology,* July 2012. In this article, "high recall frequency" is defined as on average 9.8 dreams per month, and is expected to decline with age. Not so in my case!

peoples, and everything in between[18]. The three of us reunited at the 1997 IASD conference held near Asheville, North Carolina (where Joy was living at that time), and I have attended every conference since then (with the exception of 1998), and I have presented papers at most of them. I even hosted the conference at Bridgewater State in 2006.

Participation in this organization provided me with some very useful practices, among them the ancient technique of dream incubation, in which one poses a question to be answered prior to going to sleep at night, and then records the answer upon awakening. Like the many Tarot decks described in the previous chapter, this technique "works" – at least some of the time! The philosophy upon which it rests is that the dreams, or whatever source is providing them, are essentially wiser than our waking conscious minds. This is really very similar to the ideas fundamental to the training I received in SOTGO and at the Arcane School; it relies upon contacting what the Hindu sage Patanjali referred to as the "raincloud of knowable things"[19]. Or, as John Lennon put it, "Nothing you can know that isn't KNOWN; Nothing you can see that isn't SHOWN."[20] One may receive an answer in an incubation one did not expect, one which answers a question more essential than the one asked![21]

In the summer of 2002, as the result of a dream image, I took up the crumhorn, an early Renaissance double reed instrument. This was the first time since my college years that I had played an instrument, though my wife had organized a group of recorder players several years before. One of its older members had gifted the group with an alto crumhorn, the sad, nasal sound of which I very much enjoyed. At that time, my summer archaeological field school was working in a wooded portion of the Bridgewater State campus[22]. We laid out straight transects, each of which was assigned a letter to designate it, and we excavated small square test pits at intervals along those transects. Here is the text of the dream which was my impetus to take up the instrument:

> *I need to survey in a new line of squares at the site, because we hope to find some oboes. The line is not straight, but curves off to the left. My wife helps me do this. The oboes are placed vertically in the centers of the squares. They make a particularly sad kind of music.*

---

[18] International Association for the Study of Dreams, https://www.asdreams.org/.

[19] Alice A. Bailey, *The Light of the Soul: The Yoga Sutras of Patanjali*. Lucis Publishing, New York, 1927. Book 1, Sutra 19.

[20] John Lennon and Paul McCartney, "All You Need is Love". https://www.youtube.com/watch?v=_7xMfIp-irg.

[21] Of course, not all dreams have this deep a significance. Some of them simply reflect ongoing life circumstances or concerns; others appear to be even less meaningful. In fact, I do not think that any of the many theories of dream origins is capable of covering the entire range of dream experience. Any dream might convey multiple messages which satisfy several of these theories.

[22] Curtiss Hoffman, South Brook Archaeological Survey. On file at the Massachusetts Historical Commission, Boston MA, 2003.

And here is my commentary on the dream from that time:

> *The word "oboe" is an English corruption of French haut bois, or "high wood" – in Shakespeare's time it was still spelled "hautboy"*[23]. *At this time in the dig we were at a high elevation in the woods, and the transect I was planning to survey in that day was Transect J. This letter is shaped like the curved transect in the dream, but also like a crumhorn (German "bent horn"), which, like an oboe, has a double reed.*

Within a few years, I had achieved relative mastery on this instrument, and I also acquired a soprano, tenor, and bass crumhorn and learned to play them. Once I was confident of my abilities on them, we began attending Early Music Week at Pinewoods, a summer camp run by the Country Dance and Song Society in Plymouth, Massachusetts[24]. One of the things to which I was exposed by this practice, more or less for the first time, was the wonderful world of Renaissance polyphony. Playing pieces scored for small groups of instruments with multiple cross-cutting melodic lines was inspirational for me, and it has definitely influenced my process of writing music. Most of the pieces in the *Musical Dream Tarot* incorporate polyphony, and all of them are scored for small groups of instruments. By 2011, I had graduated from the crumhorns, which have a limited range, to the dulcian, an ancestor of the modern bassoon. I currently have a tenor and an alto dulcian. With these instruments, I have played (mostly bassoon) parts in my university's wind band, as well as playing tenor and alto lines in small amateur chamber groups.

At the 2012 conference of the International Association for the Study of Dreams at Tufts University in Medford, Massachusetts, I met Lauren Schneider, and we both experienced the kind of instant affinity which I have described with Joy and Gudrun. Following a trope in the novels of fantasy author Robin Hobb,[25] I refer to this kind of affinity as "recognition of pack." I have experienced this with quite a number of other people, so I readily recognize it for what it is and I do not mistake it for any kind of romantic attachment. Lauren, who is a licensed psychotherapist, has developed a therapeutic practice using the Tarot as a focus, which she calls "Tarotpy©,"[26] and this connection rekindled my interest in the Tarot. Since that time, I have attended many of the workshops and symposia she has offered at the dream conferences, and this has had further implications for this project, as I will explain in Chapter Five.

My final impetus in the direction of this project came at the 2018 IASD conference in Scottsdale, Arizona. Here I met Carmen Sorrenti, an Italian artist who has designed her own Tarot deck from

---

[23] e.g., William Shakespeare, *Antony and Cleopatra*, ed, Louis Wright and Virginia LaMar. Washington Square Press, New York. Act 4, Scene 3.

[24] Country Dance and Song Society, https://camp.cdss.org/.

[25] Robin Hobb (Megan Lindholm), *Assassin's Quest*, Bantam Books, New York, 1997. Passim.

[26] https://www.dreamsandtarotpy.com/tarotpy.

her dreams, called the Pholarcos Tarot[27]. It was immediately obvious to me that this was another "pack" member! Carmen actually won a prize in the conference art show that year for her depiction of Key 16 – with which, as I noted above, I have a strong affinity. Her deck, too, played a role in the inception of *The Musical Dream Tarot* (see Chapter Five). Carmen has kindly given me permission to use all the images of her deck for this project.

It is not surprising that classical music finds its way into my dreams, sometimes as what Freud referred to as "day-residue"[28] as the result of having heard it recently, either from my own collection or on the radio; but sometimes unrelated to recently heard music. Using my dream database program, I was able to search for the names of composers in my dreams over the span of 29 years (1992 – 2021) prior to the inception of the Musical Dream Tarot project. The most frequent among the composers from whose music I recorded dreams were Gustav Mahler (55 dreams), Richard Wagner (37), Wolfgang Mozart (30), Ludwig van Beethoven (24), J. S. Bach (22), Franz Schubert (13), Richard Strauss (12), and Sergei Prokofiev and Pyotr Ilyich Tchaikovsky (10 each). Pieces by these nine composers accounted for 63.4% of my recorded dreams which contained recognizable music. Most of them belong to the Romantic period. An additional 26 Romantic period composers whose compositions appeared less frequently in my dreams accounted for 22.0% of the total. Earlier composers other than Bach and Mozart accounted for only 6.3% of the total, while more modern composers – none more recent than Leonard Bernstein – accounted for 8.3%. Dreams with identified classical composers constituted 2.1% of all of my dreaming from 1992 – 2021. I have recalled very few dreams featuring music by composers in other genres, such as jazz or popular music. This clearly demonstrates a stylistic preference in my dreams, which is also reflected in the Musical Dream Tarot.

At the 2022 IASD conference in Tucson, Arizona, I gave a special 90-minute presentation on this project, detailing my methodology and playing twelve of the completed Major Arcana pieces. I also provided ten of the Minor Arcana pieces as background music for the conference art show, and my wife and I dressed as the King and Queen of Pentacles at the costume Dream Ball at the end of the conference and played some excerpts from those two pieces. After my presentation, an African-American attendee asked me what the results would have been like had my musical tastes run to hip-hop or other African origin genres. I replied that there was no reason why there should be only one Musical Dream Tarot, and I encouraged her to compose her own!

---

[27] Carmen Sorrenti, *Pholarchos Tarot*, First Edition. Arnell Art, aando@arnellart.com, 2018.
[28] Sigmund Freud, *The Interpretation of Dreams*. Oxford University Press, Oxford UK, 2000.

◆ 3 ◆
The Gilgamesh Cantata

Throughout the first months of 2010, I was feeling somewhat depressed, due to the disappearance of a heart-based relationship with a former student of mine. In meditation, I received a rare direct message from Master 7 8 – who never pulled punches: "Do you realize that you are spiritually stagnating?" This was certainly a wake-up call, but at the time I had no idea what I might do to get out of that state. I would soon find out!

At that year's IASD conference, once again held in Asheville, North Carolina in June, I obtained a copy of *The Red Book*, Jung's own dream diary, which he had insisted not be published until 50 years after his death.[1] I began reading this hefty volume once I returned home from the conference, and I soon noticed some peculiarities about it. It seemed only to want to be read at night. I might awaken in the middle of the night from a dream, and recognize this as a cue to come out to my living room and, after recording the dream in my journal, do some reading in *The Red Book*. To my surprise, more than once I discovered that the dream I had just recorded was very similar to the one Jung was describing in the passage I was reading! For example, on one occasion I was having difficulty getting to sleep; I kept tossing and turning in bed, so I got up and opened the *Red Book* to the next passage I had reached, in which Jung wrote, "Sleep does not come. I toss and turn – sleep still does not come . . . It must already be midnight—and still sleep does not come."[2] At which point, I looked at a clock, and, sure enough, it was just about midnight! These kinds of synchronicities convinced me that I should pay close attention to what the book might have to offer me.

Immediately following my first summer at Pinewoods camp in August of that year, I received a commission from a "big dream" to write a vocal *a capella* cantata on a text from *The Red Book*, a series of incantations to the Mesopotamian hero Gilgamesh[3]. Jung had dreamt about this gigantic character on three successive nights in 1914. On the first night, he informed the hero that science had replaced mythology in the minds of modern people. This was a fatal blow, and Gilgamesh fell down, mortally wounded. Jung was sorry for having caused this, and he managed to persuade Gilgamesh that the latter was a fantasy. Once having done so, he condensed the giant into a tiny

---

[1] The book, which he never actually finished, is written in a Swiss dialect of German in an archaic "Fraktur" script, but it is accompanied by a good English translation in the back.
[2] Carl Gustav Jung, *The Red Book*: *Liber Novus*. Ed. and trans. Sonu Shamdasani. W.W.Norton & Company, New York, 2009. p. 262.
[3] Ibid., pp.278-285. Gilgamesh is called "Izdubar" in *The Red Book*, as the result of a then mistaken reading of the cuneiform signs which make up his name. The correction was not made until R. Campbell Thompson's 1928 critical edition of the epic.

form and placed him inside of an egg. He put the egg in his waistcoat pocket and walked to a village, where he and the villagers performed the incantations to release the god from the egg. These incantations form the vocal line for the cantata. Here is my dream text from that night:

> *I am in an open classroom on the 2nd floor of an old wood frame building at Pinewoods. The class is a choir, conducted by Sarah Mead and Sheila Beardsley. Sarah sends me downstairs to see who is there in the road. I go out the door, and there I see a middle-aged woman with an old wooden cart across the road. It is yoked to a strange large animal behind it, mostly white with light bluish patches on its muzzle and back. It appears to be either a small bull or a calf. The woman wants to bring it into the classroom. I tell her that she can't do that; the animal is too large to fit in the narrow stairway. She doesn't see that this is a problem; she transforms it into a spineless sea creature which fits onto a small plastic dinner plate, with 3 slices of yellow-green pickle on the left side. I'm surprised, but obviously she may now enter. I usher her into the classroom, holding the plate aloft in her right hand. Inside, there are about 20 students, male and female, sitting on wooden folding chairs arranged in irregular rows. Sheila counts how many of them there are, and then Sarah hands out small slips of paper to each of them, each one containing a single word. However, standing in the back of the room, I get a larger piece which contains the entire text. I compare my text with the slips given to the other students and I reach the conclusion that they are in total the same as what I have. I see that the text is the Izdubar invocation from Jung's Red Book, and that it also contains an image of the bull calf and the cart. I'm surprised that the image is the same as what I saw on the street. The text is in both Fraktur German and English, at the same time. Sarah asks each student to sing their word, in order from the front to the back of the room, while I read the entire text silently to check that it has been read correctly. The first word, in much larger size print, appears to be "Einkauf" or "Einkampf". I'm really uncertain about my role here.*

Sarah and Sheila were the directors of the Early Music Week activities at the camp that summer. The image of the bull does in fact appear in *The Red Book*, a few pages before the point I'd reached in it at that time[4]. "Einkauf" (purchase) and "Einkampf" (struggle) turned out to be predictive of the fate of this composition.

My initial reaction to this "commission" was to affirm the sense of uncertainty with which the dream ended: "I don't know how to do that!" After all, it had been more than 45 years since I'd last written any music. The response, in a subsequent dream, was "We will show you!" And "they" – whoever "they" are – did. The themes for this work were entirely based on my dreams over an 18-month period, a total of 132 dreams. As my academic training had involved the study

---

[4] Ibid., p. 127.

of ancient Mesopotamian languages as well as archaeology, I was able to translate the Swiss-German text of this part of *The Red Book* directly into Babylonian Akkadian, the language of the best-known version of the Gilgamesh Epic,[5] for this work, entitled *The Gilgamesh Cantata*. This language has been effectively dead for over 2,300 years, known only to a very small number of Middle Eastern scholars like myself. But it is a beautiful, mellifluous language, with many u-vowels, ideal for singing. It may be the case that my translation is the first extended text written in this language since the time of Alexander the Great!

Writing a cantata was not something I had ever envisioned doing before, and to prepare for it I audited a number of undergraduate music theory and orchestration courses at my university. One of the instructors, Dr. Stephen Young, kindly agreed to have the small chorus which he directed perform two of the completed movements of this eight-movement work at a public concert in the Spring of 2012. I also presented on the entire 47-minute long work at the 2012 IASD conference, with computer-synthesized excerpts of all of the movements; and at the subsequent Boston area regional conference at Regis College in Weston, MA, I and five other singers actually performed two of the eight movements live for the audience.

The tunes which make up the movements of the *Gilgamesh Cantata* may be divided into four types:

1. <u>Tunes within Dreams</u>: these are pieces of music which were embedded within the action of the dream itself, either as heard music or as my viewing of scores, or both.

2. <u>Whole Dream Tunes</u>: These pieces constitute the entire text of the dream. It is possible that some of them were all that I was able to remember of a longer dream, but some of them were certainly nothing more than the tune itself.

3. <u>Hypnopompic Tunes</u>: Upon partial awakening, I usually rehearsed the dream in my mind while in a semi-lucid state, and a musical phrase might accompany this recollection. This state of consciousness is referred to in dream literature as "hypnopompic", or leading out of the dream, as opposed to "hypnagogic"[6], which leads into the dream.

4. <u>Referential Dreams</u>: These were dreams in which I was given instructions on how to combine dream tunes, how to organize the movements, and how to have them performed, but did not contain any actual music.

The predominant type in the set of 132 dreams was the Referential type, making up nearly half of the total. Next were Whole Dream tunes, with close to a quarter of the total. The frequency of Tunes within Dreams and of Hypnopompic Tunes was fairly low, at about 1/6 of the total each.

---

[5] R. Campbell Thompson, *The Gilgamesh Epic*. Luzac and Co., London, UK., 1928.
[6] Robert Van DeCastle, *Our Dreaming Mind*. Ballantine Books, New York, 1995.

These percentages are shown in Figure 3.1 below:

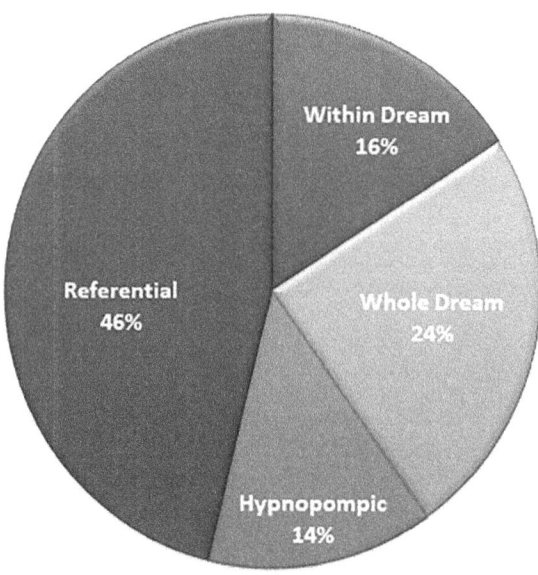

Figure 3.1: Gilgamesh Cantata Dream Types

However, 31 of the referential dreams occurred after the completion of the work. If these are subtracted from the total, the percentages of the four types are closer to equal, as shown in Figure 3.2, although hypnopompic dreams were still the least frequent:

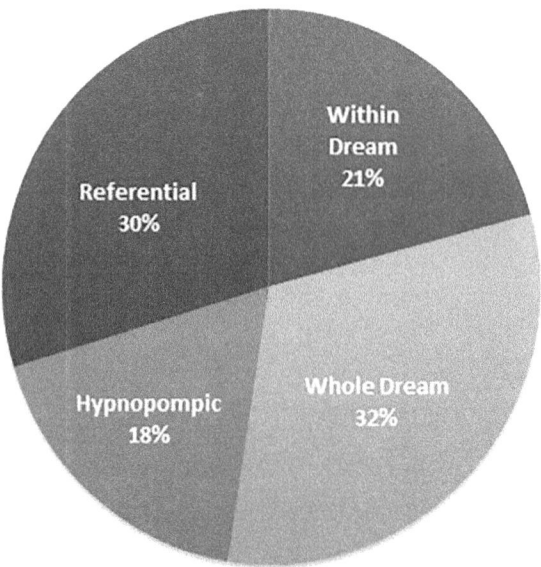

Figure 3.2: Pre-Completion Gilgamesh Cantata Dream Types

All of the music in the cantata is original music from my dreams, with one notable exception. In the fifth movement, in which the text describes the anticipation of the villagers awaiting the reemergence of the god from the egg, a series of interpretive dreams instructed me to incorporate into the music the final chorale from J. S. Bach's *St. Matthew Passion*, "Wir sitzen uns mit Traenen nieder"[7], using my Akkadian translation of Jung's text. The text of Bach's chorale is very similar to Jung's text – perhaps it even influenced his own dreaming.

At that time, I had hopes to publish the cantata and have it more widely performed. What I didn't realize was that the Bridgewater concert was recorded, without my knowledge or consent, and put on the university's YouTube channel – from which it was exported to YouTube generally. The Jung Institute, which holds the patent on Jung's writings, found out about it and threatened to sue the university for copyright infringement – even though the work was translated into another (dead) language. Over the previous summer, I had made the acquaintance of Jung's grandson Andreas, and at his invitation I actually visited the house near Zurich which Jung had built for his residence and psychoanalytic practice, and where Andreas still lives. I even played for him electronic versions of two of the movements. Andreas attempted to intercede on my behalf with the Jung Institute, and the result was that while the YouTube video was taken down, the Institute withdrew their suit and agreed to allow performances, but not recordings, of the work. I have since tried to interest several choral groups in it, but so far this has not led to any further performances. That certainly explains "Einkauf" and "Einkampf"!

Following this initial burst of creative endeavor, I was inspired to begin a number of additional compositions, also based on my dreams. They include a threnody for my mother for string quartet, a clarinet-piano duet, and a dulcian concerto – all unfinished. But then I became involved in completing a number of large-scale archaeological projects which distracted my energy away from musical dreams, and this resulted in a creative dry spell which lasted from 2013 – 2021. I continued to receive music in my dreams occasionally, and to record it in my dream journal, but without any inspiration to create particular compositions.

At the 2018 IASD conference, I attended a workshop given by David Low, in which he recounted an experience he had had in which a long series of spiritually inspired dreams was followed by a period without any such content, and he suggested that this might be a phenomenon characteristic of the spiritual path. I compared his experience with mine, and I felt that this might be the case for me: that the Spirit descended for that one short burst of creative energy, which lasted about two years in all, and then it withdrew. I was resigned to this, though I missed the creative energy which had characterized the writing of the *Gilgamesh Cantata*.

---

[7] Johann Sebastian Bach, *The Saint Matthew Passion*. https://www.youtube.com/watch?v=Tq4lxMcwYwU. #68 (2:41:00 – 2:46:47).

◆ 4 ◆
The Origins of the Project

At the 2021 IASD conference, which was held entirely on-line via Zoom© due to the COVID epidemic, I attended another Tarot workshop facilitated by Lauren Schneider, at which she invited participants to frame a question to which they wanted an answer, and then to choose two Tarot cards from any deck we had at our disposal, in hard copy or on-line. We were then dispatched in groups of three to virtual breakout rooms to work on these cards, as if they were our dreams. I had recently nearly completed work on what I knew would be my last two major archaeological reports, so, using Carmen Sorrenti's Pholarchos Tarot deck[1], which was the only complete one I had at my disposal at the time, I posed the following question to the Tarot cards: "What is my next project?" The cards I drew were the Trail of Sparks and the Two of Sparks, which correspond to the Knight of Wands and the Two of Wands in a traditional deck.[2]

Figure 4.1: Tarot Cards Drawn in Answer to My Question

---

[1] Carmen Sorrenti, op. cit.

[2] The Pholarchos Tarot substitutes Sparks, Spirals, Wings, and Coral for the traditional Wands, Cups, Swords, and Pentacles – it is by no means the only deck to diverge creatively from these names. While the Trail of Sparks in the Pholarcos Tarot is in greyscale as shown here (as are the other three Trails as well as the four Aces), all of the other images are in color. The color versions of the images are reproduced on the website (www.musicaldreamtarot.com) which complements this volume.

The first card, once the group worked on it, seemed to relate primarily to my fostering of the preceding archaeological projects. The second card didn't give me an immediate answer, but it did seem to point in a hopeful future direction, with its message of "potency", its Aries symbols, and its two horses – which we interpreted as steeds that could get me to my destination.

About a week after the conference, I received my copy of Lauren's excellent new book on Tarot, *Tarotpy©: It's All in the Cards*[3]. As I noted in Chapter Two, I have attended many of her Tarot workshops at IASD conferences, and as a result I am very familiar with her methods. This made for a quick read of the book, which includes a number of practical exercises for readers to undertake to familiarize themselves with the methodology she has developed.

While exchanging email with Lauren about the book, I suggested that one final exercise she could have included in it was to "design your own Tarot deck," thinking of Carmen Sorrenti's work to do just that. I admitted to her that I do not have the artistic capability to do this, as my creative talents, such as they are, lie in the field of music. After I sent the email, I suddenly realized that this was the answer to the question I had posed to the cards: I was being tasked with writing music for the Tarot, based on themes derived from my dreams. This, indeed, became my "next project"! The first dream with music for the Tarot occurred on June 24th of that year, the night after I had the realization that this was my next project.

I realized at the outset that this would be a very large undertaking, but I have had continued faith that the dreams would bring me what I need to complete it, and I have not been disappointed. As St. Paul observed, "Faith is the substance of things hoped for, the evidence of things not seen." [4] I also would like to make it clear that, from the outset, my intention in undertaking this project has consistently been one of *service* – service to all those who use the Tarot, for whatever purpose. Service was the keynote of all of the work we did in SOTGO, and it is also the keynote of all of the Arcane School work[5]. I have had a motivation to serve others from early in my teenage years, and indeed it was the emphasis on service which was my main motivation for joining SOTGO. It is clear from the esoteric teachings that service is the key that opens the door to higher states of consciousness, or as Christ said, "Give, and it shall be given unto you."[6] Giving without expectation of personal gain opens one to impression from higher spiritual sources, as an affirmation from the opening of many of the SOTGO rituals states: "Let the pure stream of cosmic consciousness flow in me and through me unimpeded." My decades-long practice of service meditation certainly prepared me to be such a vehicle for the music of the Tarot, but I must emphasize that the tunes which make it up are NOT mine, and derive from a Source whose specific identity is unknown to

---

[3] Lauren Schneider, *Tarotpy©: It's All in the Cards*. New Insights Press, Los Angeles CA, 2021.
[4] Hebrews 11:1.
[5] Alice A. Bailey, *The Consciousness of the Atom*. Lucis Publishing, New York, 1922. p. 28.
[6] Luke 6:38.

me, but which is full of wisdom and which has anticipated every stage of this complex project with an uncanny precision.

I also believe that it is not a coincidence that it was not until the final reports on those archaeological projects were complete and ready to be sent off for publication that I was in a position to ask, and to receive an answer to, the question I posed to the Tarot cards mentioned at the outset of this chapter. In effect, completing those projects "cleared the decks" (pun intended!) for me to undertake something new, which would require the devotion of a great deal of time and effort – day and night – to it. The results have indeed been surprising, with a total of 778 dreams devoted to this project since the 2021 dream conference.

One of the things the practice of archaeology has inculcated in me is the importance of careful record-keeping. Thus, in addition to the qualitative, artistic aspect of this project, which is inspired by the dreams, I also include a good deal of quantitative data in the next three chapters, as a demonstration of how the project was shaped. In preparing for this, I have followed a set of guidelines in the Tibetan teacher's *A Treatise on White Magic*, which provides a series of fifteen rules for bringing an idea into manifestation.[7] Slightly more than half of my dreams since the 2021 conference (50.4%) have had a direct connection to this music, either as actual tunes heard or as references to the project.

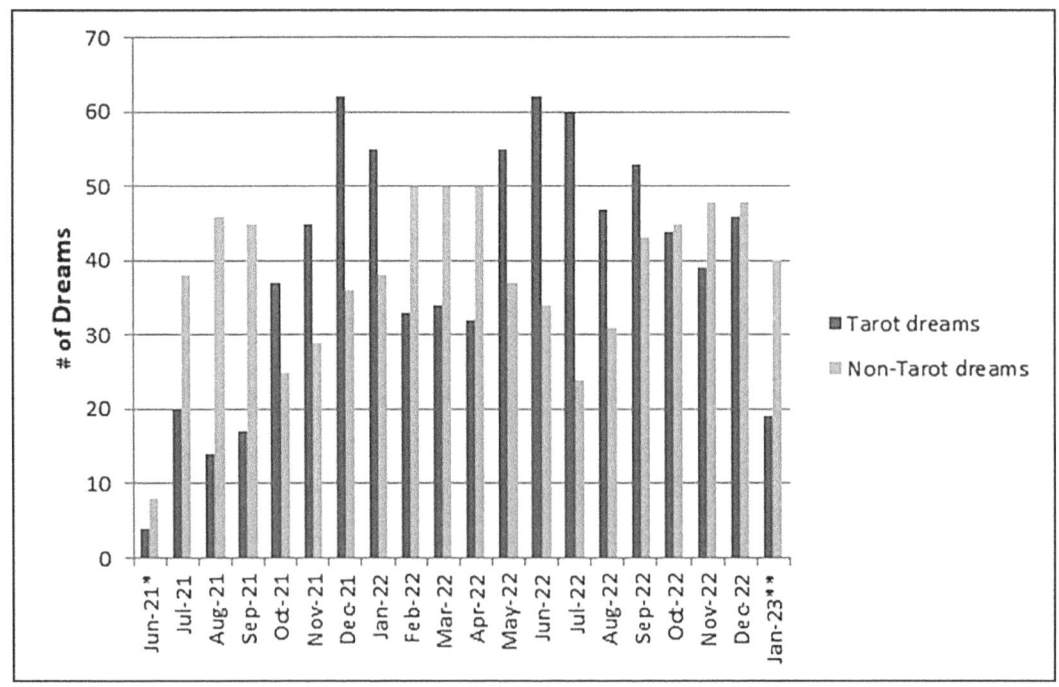

Figure 4.2: Monthly Tabulation of Tarot and Non-Tarot Dreams

---

[7] Alice A. Bailey, *A Treatise on White Magic*. Lucis Publishing, New York, 1934. pp. xii-xiv.

Figure 4.2 (opposite) compares the frequency of these dreams to that of dreams about other subjects, month by month.[8] It is evident from this graph that the project got off to a slow start over the first three months, but that by October of 2021 the pace had picked up markedly, and reached a peak in December and January of that year. It declined a bit through April, but then picked up again from May through July of 2022, before declining to a more moderate level thereafter. There was a drastic fall-off in January of 2023, after I had completed work on the last of the Keys. The final date on which I received any music related to the project was January 25th, 2023 – almost exactly 19 months since the first dream. With the exception of that month, there were at least 30 dreams related to the Tarot In every month since September, 2021. The maxima, in December of 2021 and June of 2022, were 62 dreams, on average two dreams per night. In fact, once the project began to pick up steam, there were only a few nights in which a Tarot-related dream was absent. In all, I have had Tarot-related dreams on average on 79.9% of the nights from June 24th of 2021 to January 25th, 2023, sometimes with multiple dreams on the same night, as shown in Figure 4.3 below:

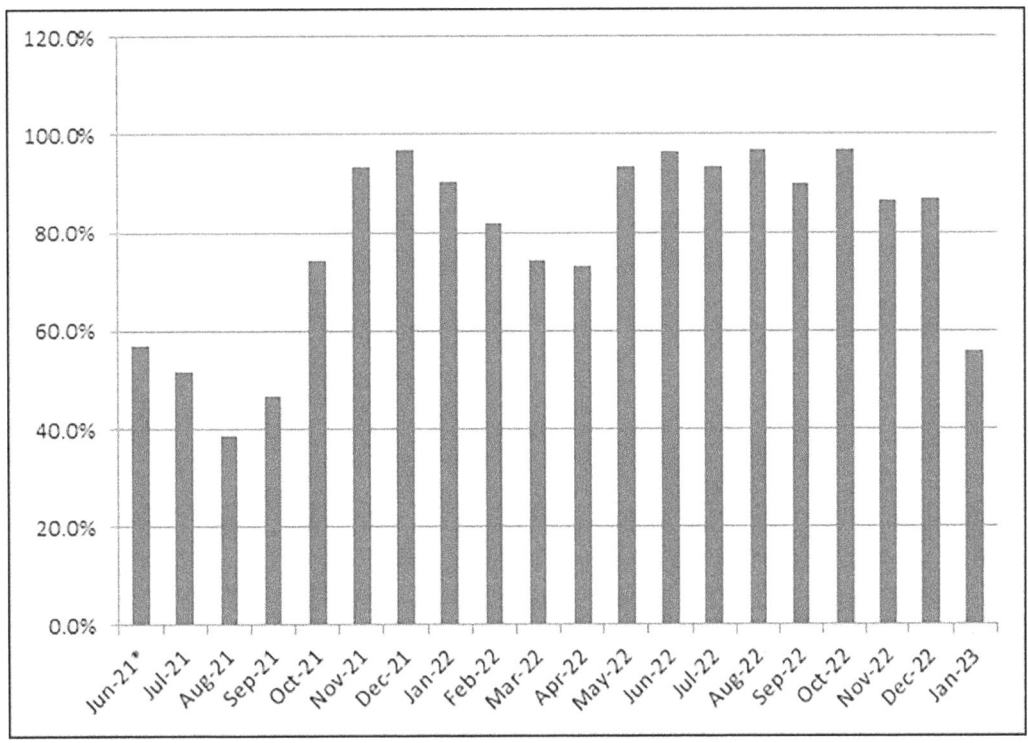

Figure 4.3: Percentage of Nights Containing Tarot Dreams, by Month

---

[8] Because the first dream of the series was on June 24th, 2021, that month's records only represent the final week. As the dreams ended on January 25th, 2023, the final week of that month is not included. This will be the case for all of the graph lines for those two months which follow in the next two chapters.

This graph has a similar configuration to the one above, with a slow start-up during the first few months, and a decline from February through April of 2022 and a sharp decline in January of 2023. However, in no month from October of 2021 through December of 2023 did the percentage of the nights which contained Tarot-related dreams drop below 73%. In December of 2021, and in June, August, and October of 2022, it reached a maximum of 97% – that is, there was only one night during those months in which there was not a Tarot-related dream. This is a much higher intensity than what I experienced when writing the Gilgamesh Cantata, by a factor of about six. I will report further on the actual results of this process in Chapters Six and Seven.

Below is an example of a raw tune derived from a dream, as recorded in my journal:

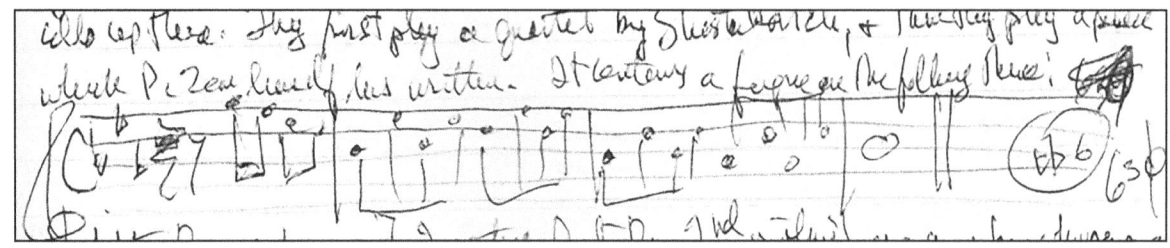

Figure 4.4: Eb Tune #6

And here is how this tune was incorporated into a larger piece, the music for the Four of Cups:

Figure 4.5: Segment of the Score for the Four of Cups

• 5 •
The Matrix

One of the few human universals, which as Lévi-Strauss has shown[1] is found even among so-called "savage" cultures, is our propensity to project order and structure onto the universe. This order often includes a mapping of the heavens, onto which our cultural ideas and images are projected. As Lévi-Strauss wrote, "The cosmographic code is no truer than any other; and it is no better, except from the methodological point of view, as far as its operations can be checked from without."[2] The degree to which these systems of thought correlate with external observations is to a certain degree a factor in their longevity and transmissibility to other cultures. However, as always with these cultural systems, we are confronted with a dialectic between inner and outer realities, in which the inner sometimes predominates over the outer. This is not to say that one is "truer" than the other; they simply reflect different realities.

For example, due to the Precession of the Equinoxes, which is caused by the wobble of the Earth's axis, for the past 2,000 years or so the constellation Aries can no longer be seen rising at sunrise starting on the day of the Spring Equinox, yet it remains the first of the astrological signs and is still assigned to March-April. Nor are the stars which comprise this constellation, or most of the others, anywhere near one another in space; they only appear to be so from the perspective of an Earth observer. While I acknowledge the prospect that there are actual celestial influences, and that they may be coming our way along vectors ("rays") in space from outside of our solar system, I believe that it is from these directional locations, rather than from specific stars which appear to us in those directions, that they are affecting us in subtle ways, many of which appear to be deeply engrained in our unconscious. Even the Tibetan teacher Djwahl Kuhl, the author of a treatise on esoteric astrology, warned students: "Seek not to work out hypotheses of alignment based on the physical planets. The truth lies not there."[3]

As a further example of this, in 2006 I did a study of my own dreams in which there were themes of conflicted travel, finance, or communications – all of these themes traditionally linked in astrology to times when the planet Mercury – which is said to affect all three of these conditions[4] – is in "retrograde".[5] Even though I had not paid much attention before to dreams in "Mercury retrograde"

---

[1] Claude Levi-Strauss, *The Savage Mind*. University of Chicago Press, Chicago IL, 1966. Passim.
[2] Ibid., *The Raw and the Cooked*. Harper and Row, New York, 1969. p. 240.
[3] Alice A. Bailey, *Letters on Occult Meditation*. Lucis Publishing, New York, 1922. p.6.
[4] https://www.astrology.com/planets/mercury.
[5] Factually, Mercury has the most circular orbit of any of the planets, but from the perspective of an Earth observer it appears to track backwards in the heavens for about 21 days, about 3 times a year.

periods, I found that there was a statistically strong correlation between dreams with these three themes and those times, and that they were relatively absent during times when Mercury was "direct". At the time, I was teaching a course entitled Culture and Consciousness, in which the students – only one of whom was conversant in astrology – were asked to keep dream journals. Halfway through the "retrograde" period which fell within that semester, I announced the results of my study to the class and asked them to note any similar dream correlations in their journals. At the end of the semester I collected the journals and tabulated the results. I did a split-half test, between the periods before and after I made the announcement, and I found that the prevalence of "Mercury retrograde" type dreams was statistically constant throughout the retrograde period for these students, whether or not they were aware of the phenomenon. This suggests that one need not be conscious of the symbolic associations of astrology to be affected by them!

I mention this because what follows in this chapter, and throughout the rest of the book, relies upon one particularly robust system of thought and cosmology which derives ultimately from the so-called "Axial Era" in the eastern Mediterranean basin[6], in which the more ancient philosophies of Mesopotamia, Egypt, Persia, Israel, and Greece were blended together into a more or less integrated model. This overarching model, whether it was fully realized in the form of the Tarot images during the Axial Era itself (as suggested in Chapter One) or crystallized as the result of its resurgence during the Renaissance, forms the basis of the Tarot. As the 19th century occultist Eliphas Levi wrote, "an imprisoned person with no other book than the Tarot, if he knew how to use it, could in a few years acquire universal knowledge, and would be able to speak on all subjects with unequalled learning and inexhaustible eloquence."[7] This system provided me with a coherent matrix for assigning particular dream tunes to specific Tarot cards.

Through my study and practice of Western esotericism, I have been familiar with the Major Arcana as meditation seeds for many decades, and I am well aware of the existence of several systems of assigning these 22 Keys to astrological signs and planets, and to the 22 letters of the Hebrew alphabet. In the version of the system I learned in SOTGO, which is based upon *Sefer Yetzirah*, a principal source of Jewish mysticism,[8] twelve of the Keys (#s 4, 5, 6, 7, 8, 9, 11, 13, 14, 15, 17, and 18) are assigned to the zodiacal signs from Aries through Pisces, respectively. Each of these is associated with a particular "quality", among other correspondences. Seven of the remaining Keys (#s 1, 2, 3, 10, 16, 19, and 21) are assigned to the visible planets: Mercury, the Moon, Venus, Jupiter, Mars, the Sun, and Saturn, respectively. These are considered dual in nature, and thus have pairs of opposed qualities.

---

[6] From ca. 600 B.C. – 200 A.D. as posited by Karl Jaspers, *The Origin and Goal of History*. Routledge Revivals, Milton Park, UK, 2011. p. 2.

[7] Eliphas Levi (Alphonse Louis Constant), *The Key to the Mysteries*. Martino Fine Books, Eastford CT, 2013.

[8] Aryeh Kaplan, op.cit.

The remaining three Keys (#s 0, 12, and 20) are assigned to three of the alchemical elements: Air, Water, and Fire, respectively[9]. No specific qualities are associated with these three Keys. Each of these 22 cards is associated with a particular type of "intelligence". Each of the zodiacal signs is also associated with one of the four classical elements: Fire (Aries, Leo, Sagittarius); Water (Cancer, Scorpio, Pisces); Air (Gemini, Libra, Aquarius); and Earth (Taurus, Virgo, Capricorn), as are the planets (ordinarily to two elements, except for Sun and Moon). Thus, each of the Tarot Keys is associated with one or more of the four elements.

It should be noted that the formulation of the widely used system of Western musical theory and notation was also taking place in northern Italy at exactly the same time that the Tarot was popularized there.[10] And, like the Tarot, the theoretical basis of the 12-tone system used (or intentionally disused as in the serial music of the early 20th century) was retrojected onto a conjectured Greek antecedent[11]. It is therefore not coincidental that the twelve keys of the diatonic scale have been made to correspond to the twelve zodiacal signs, starting with C major for Aries and continuing up the chromatic scale to B major for Pisces.[12] Many of the 16th century theorists, not least among them Johannes Kepler[13], believed in the Pythagorean concept of the "music of the spheres": the idea that each of the planets expresses a musical note in a harmonious concert. Thus, the relationship between astrology and music was already formulated at that time, and echoes of this idea can still be found in more recent esoteric literature.[14]

The compositions derived from dreams which I assigned to the twelve zodiacal Keys of the Major Arcana are all scored in only one musical key, though some may alternate between the major and the relative minor of that key, or to the major key corresponding to that minor[15]. In addition, each of the zodiacal signs is considered to have one or two planetary "rulers", and these associations were used to attribute up to two musical keys to the planetary Keys. Each of the remaining three Keys, as well as Key 2 (Water), and Keys 3 and 21 (Earth), is associated with an element, for which there are potentially three associated astrological signs and musical keys. Thus, for musical

---

[9] Some 20th century astrologers assign them to the outer planets (Uranus, Neptune, and Pluto, respectively – never mind that Pluto has since been demoted to the status of a "dwarf planet").

[10] Anne Smith, *The Performance of 16th Century Music: Learning from the Theorists.* Oxford University Press, Oxford UK, 2011. pp. 4-18.

[11] While there were Greek names given by Aristotle to eight of the twelve modes (e.g., Phrygian, Lydian, etc.), the Renaissance theorists added four more to fit them into the larger structure. Ibid., pp. 88-101.

[12] To avoid confusion, I am using throughout the book the capitalized word "Keys" to refer to the Tarot cards, and the uncapitalized word "keys" to refer to the musical keys of the diatonic scale.

[13] Johannes Kepler, *The Harmony of the World*. Translated by Aiton, E. J.; Duncan, A. M.; and Field, J. American Philosophical Society, Philadelphia, PA. 1997.

[14] e.g. Alice Bailey, *Letters on Occult Meditation*, op.cit., pp.55-56.

[15] e.g., a composition in Eb major has C minor as its relative minor, so C major could also be used.

compositions associated with the planetary Keys, there might be music in two different musical keys, for example D (Gemini) and F (Virgo) for Key 1, The Magician (Mercury)[16]. For the elemental Keys, there might be three keys, for example Eb (Cancer), G (Scorpio), and B (Pisces) for Key 12, The Hanged Man (Water). This matrix provided me with the basics for assigning the pieces to Tarot Keys by their musical keys, as shown in Figure 5.1 below:

Key #	Name	Attribution	Ruler	Major Key
0	The Fool	Uranus/Air		D,F#,Bb
1	The Magician	Mercury/Air		D,F
2	The High Priestess	Moon/Water		Eb,G,B
3	The Empress	Venus/Earth		C#,F#,F
4	The Emperor	Aries	Mars	C
5	The Hierophant	Taurus	Venus	C#
6	The Lovers	Gemini	Mercury	D
7	The Chariot	Cancer	Moon	Eb
8	Strength	Leo	Sun	E
9	The Hermit	Virgo	Mercury	F
10	The Wheel of Fortune	Jupiter		Ab,B
11	Justice	Libra	Venus	F#
12	The Hanged Man	Neptune/Water		Eb,G,B
13	Death	Scorpio	Pluto/Mars	G
14	Temperance	Sagittarius	Jupiter	G#
15	The Devil	Capricorn	Saturn	A
16	The Tower	Mars/Fire		C,G
17	The Star	Aquarius	Uranus/Saturn	Bb
18	The Moon	Pisces	Neptune/Jupiter	B
19	The Sun	Sun/Fire		C,E,Ab
20	Judgement	Pluto/Fire		C,E,Ab
21	The World	Saturn/Earth		C#,F,A

Figure 5.1: Assignment of Major Arcana to Musical keys

The modern Western orchestra is similarly divided into four major family groupings: Brass, Strings, Woodwinds, and Percussion. This was a further guide for orchestrating specific dream music in association with the elemental Keys, including the Minor Arcana by suit, with Brass as Fire,

---

[16] Paul Foster Case (op.cit.,passim) gives single keys for the planetary and elemental Keys, based upon a color schema associated with the Sephiroth of the Tree of Life. However, I found this limiting harmonically, and employed the attributions above.

Strings as Water, Woodwinds as Air, and Percussion as Earth, as shown in Figure 5.2 below, using the abbreviations A, K, Q, N, and P for Aces, Kings, Queens, Knights, and Pages, respectively:

Instrument	Major Arcana	Wands	Cups	Swords	Pentacles
flute	0,1,6,17(2)			A,2,3,4,5,6,7,8,9,10,K,Q,N,P	
oboe	0,1,6,7,17(2)			A,2,4,5,7,8,Q,P	
English horn	1,6,10			7,10	
clarinet	0,1,6,11,14,17(2),21			A,2,3,4,5,6,7,8,9,10,K,Q,N,P	
bassoon	0,1,6,11,17(2)			2,3,4,5,7,8,9,10,K,Q,P	
horn	4(2),10,14,19,20,21	A,3,4,5,6,7,8,9,10,K(2),Q			
trumpet	4(2),8(2),10,14,16,19,20(2)	2,3(2),4,5,6,7(2),8,9,10,K,Q,N,P			
trombone	4,14,16,19,20	A,2,3,4,5,6,7,8,9,10,K,Q,N,P			
euphonium	4,8(2),15,16,20	3,9,10,K,Q			
tuba	4,14,19	5			
violin	2(2),12(2),13(2),18(2)		A,2,3,4(2),5,6,7,8,9(2),10,K,Q,N,P		
viola	2,10,12,13,18,21		2,3,4,5,6,7,8,9,10,K,N		
cello	2,7,10,12,13,18		A,2,3,4,5,6,7,8,9,10,K,Q,N,P		
double bass			10		
glockenspiel	9				A,9,K,Q,N
vibraphone	5,9,15				A,2,3,K,N,P
harp	21				2,5,6,9,10
guitar	10		A		2,3,Q,P
piano	3,5,7,15				4,8,9,K,Q
xylophone	15				8,9
marimba	9,14				A,3,4,7,8,N,P
snare drum	4,14	4,6,7,K			9
bass drum	4,5	K			9
timpani	1,13	Q			K,N
maracas	15	10			
hand cymbals	19			9	
chimes	1,5				A,9
cymbals	13	K			
harmonium		P			
triangle		10		5	6
bongos				9	

Figure 5.2: Instruments Used for Musical Dream Tarot Keys

I took a few liberties in selecting instruments, usually assigning plucked string instruments such as harp and guitar, as well as keyboard instruments (piano, marimba, vibraphone, xylophone, and glockenspiel) to the percussion section. I used my intuition, my "inner ear", to determine which instruments to choose within the larger instrument families, mostly keeping within the same family for each piece. There are a few cases shown in which an instrument from a different grouping complements the majority which are assigned to an element[17]. These additions tended to be specified in the dreams.

At first, I thought that I was writing music for only the 22 Major Arcana, with which I am very familiar; and as a result of this familiarity I had little difficulty in assigning specific tunes intuitively to specific Keys. But several months into the project, I began to realize that I was being given more musical themes in the keys of C, F, D, G, and Bb than could possibly fit into the musical compositions for their associated Major Arcana. A possible reason for this is that almost all of the Renaissance pieces I play tend to be in these keys, especially in F and C; it was only later, starting in the Baroque period, that composers branched out into key signatures more distant in tonality from C major. This predominance is shown in Figure 5.3 below.

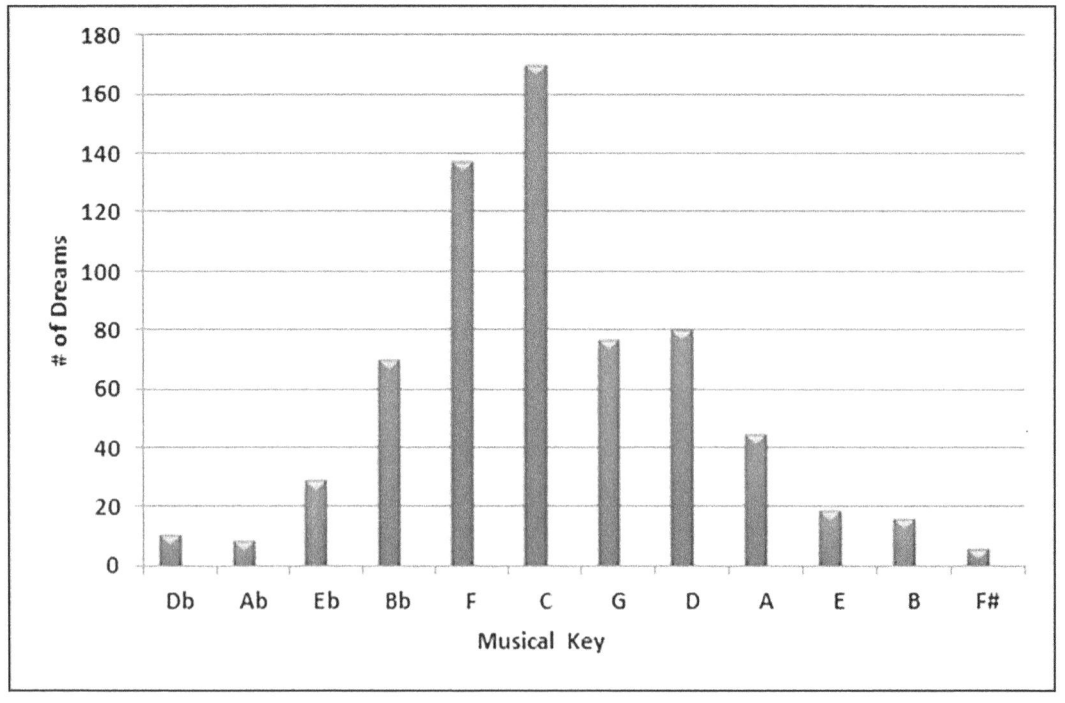

Figure 5.3: Musical Keys in Tarot Dreams

---

[17] With only five exceptions for the Major Arcana (Keys 7, 10, 14, 15, and 21), and none for the Minor Arcana, all of the cross-family additions are of percussion instruments.

By late November of 2021, I concluded that the only way to make use of all of these themes would be to create music for the 56 Minor Arcana as well. This obviously increased the scope of the project almost threefold! In addition to the Major Arcana, each of the Minor Arcana suits is also associated with one of the four elements: Wands (Fire), Cups (Water), Swords (Air), and Pentacles (Earth). Since I am not nearly as familiar with these as I am with the Major Arcana, my method of assigning music to Keys was initially different. I transcribed the music as being in a particular key, as usual, and once I had at least 14 musical selections for a suit, I laid out the 14 Minor Arcana for that suit and used the imagery of the associated dream texts to assign them to Tarot Keys. For these attributions, I also used the verbal significations of the Minor Arcana derived from the standard Rider/Waite deck[18], the Paul Foster Case deck,[19] and the Pholarchos Tarot[20]. The idea of extracting the association from the dream imagery was itself given to me in a dream:

> *I reenter a preceding dream. I see that all of the notes on the staff have turned into purple nasturtiums. I become lucid, and I realize that this has given me a key for attributing tunes to specific Minor Arcana cards, by looking for clues in the text of the dream.*

In some cases, this attribution was fairly direct: for example, most of the dreams which featured kings were associated with the King cards of their suits. A few of the attributions were extremely clear from the dream text, as in the following example:

> *I have been canvassing door-to-door for the adoption of ranked choice voting in Ashland town elections. I have been pretty successful in our neighborhood in convincing residents to vote for this in Town Meeting, and I have nearly met my quota of calls. My supervisor sends me out again with a list of just 4 more names. One of these is a man named P. Zev. My supervisor tells me that this man has led an interesting life. He ran away from home several times as a teenager, and was placed in an institution, from which he also escaped. Now he has no actual home, but lives in a horse stable. I go to the stable, which is on the right side of Chestnut Street in a less developed area. P. Zev is a youngish man with long dark hair, rather handsome. He has been grooming a brown horse. I explain the voting system to him, and he seems receptive, and agrees to vote for it. After completing my short list, I return home. My wife and I have tickets to a chamber concert this afternoon, in a small auditorium. The tickets include a small golden ball. I go to the auditorium just before the doors open to check on its location. The concierge announces that the doors are now open, and people begin to enter. I show him our tickets and the ball, but he points out that my wife has not signed her ticket, so I have to go home to*

---

[18] Arthur E. Waite, op. cit.
[19] Paul Foster Case, op. cit.
[20] Carmen Sorrenti, op. cit.

get her to do this. We return together and we are admitted. We look for our seats, which are T1 and T2, on the right side of the auditorium. These are rather good seats – the rows are labeled alphabetically from back to front – but they are already occupied. We show our stubs to an usher, who says that we are in the wrong section. We need to go to the Green Section on the left side of the hall. These seats are not quite so good. My wife has brought an ice cream cup, and when she's finished it I crush it, which makes a noise. But other people are conversing so loudly that it can hardly be heard. The red curtain on stage goes up, but behind it is another curtain, and then another. The musicians are actually on the floor in front of the stage, but the noise from the audience is so loud, even after the usher asks them to stop, that they clamber up on stage instead. They are a string quartet, and to my surprise P. Zev is the cellist. He has some difficulty hauling his cello up to the stage. They first play a string quartet by Shostakovich, and then a piece written by P. Zev himself, which includes a lively fugue.[21] I notice that the 2nd violinist is a young boy who plays a very small violin. After the performance, I go up to the players, and P. Zev recognizes me and introduces me to the others as a local political activist. I say, "In addition to that, I am a composer; I have written music for the 78 Tarot Keys from my dreams." The violist, a young man with a red beard, says, "No f---ing way!" I reply, "Yes f---ing way!" I ask P. Zev if he originally scored his piece for the small violin, and he says that he did. Later, my wife and I are in a room with several other concert attendees, discussing the new work. One woman says that it would really have been more proper to introduce the fugue theme at the beginning and then develop it. I say, "Not necessarily" as I begin to attach the slide of a brass trombone to the main part of the instrument.

My comments on this lengthy dream with an embedded tune at the time were as follows:

This long, complicated dream has some day residue elements in it. To be admitted to the English Country Dance we had attended the previous night, we had to sign off (electronically) on a COVID-19 release form. En route to the dance hall, we had gotten some ice cream cups, and my wife had finished hers after I did and I disposed of them. PZEV is the name of the engine in her Subaru. The concierge was actually Graham Chapman from the Monty Pythons. That show also featured multiple red curtains raised in sequence. There actually are small violins like the one the boy was playing, used for training young musicians - but not likely for a performance of this sort. I would interpret "f---ing" as "fugueing", and there was a way to do this with the 3½ bar phrase I recalled from the dream.

---

[21] This theme is the one shown in Figures 4.4 and 4.5, supra. The other three themes, two of which appear in the score segment, derived from earlier dreams.

The tune was in C minor, so it obviously went with the Four of Cups - appropriately, as it is for a string quartet! The number four also appears earlier in the dream, in the list of names.

In a few cases, a subsequent dream from the same night helped to associate a tune with a key, for example:

> 1) *There is a tyrant who is seeking to expand his control from his base on an island in a large river to countries upstream, including mine. We are concerned about this, and we want to take steps to prevent it. We first need to evaluate the strength of his forces, so we send our ships down the river. I am in command of 4 small ships of the sort we have used to conduct trade, and we are in the front of the flotilla, while our larger warships hang back. We come around a bend in the river, from which we can see the island. I count the number of his vessels. The commander of our warships sends me a signal asking if he should proceed to attack. I send a signal back that the tyrant's fleet is too strong for that. We will just pretend to be traders while we gather more information. This is associated with a tune.*

> 2) *I reenter the preceding dream, only now it is a game of solitaire with 2 decks of cards. I am motivated to play a bright red Jack of Hearts on one of the Tens of Hearts showing on the game board.*

The tune in the first dream was in G major, which goes with Cups, and the second dream clearly indicated that the Knight (Jack) of Cups card was to be chosen. The second dream (and a subsequent exact repeat of it from the same night) was counted as a referential dream.

However, some of these associations turned out to be deceptive; for example, the following dream, early in the process of assigning music to the Minor Arcana, seemed to point directly at the Eight of Swords:

> *Something is affecting my vision, such that I see everything double. A friend shows me a wooden stick, about 1½ inches long, in the street, but with both eyes open I see 2 sticks. With only one eye open I see only one. He shows me an Eight of Spades card, and close up my vision is single. This is associated with a descending musical scale.*

The scale was in B minor, the relative minor of D major, which certainly could go with Swords (Air). However, the tune turned out not to be for the Eight of Swords, but to be an introduction to the music for Key 6, The Lovers – assigned to Gemini, also an Air sign.

A minority of these dreams, 130 (16.7%), were of a type that had no recalled content other than the music itself. These are the equivalent of the "Whole Dream" type I experienced when I was writing the Gilgamesh Cantata. In these cases, once I had established attributions based on imagery for each of the Minor Arcana, I tried to match the melodic and rhythmic structure of the tune to others with descriptive dream texts which had enabled me to assign the tune to a Key. This percentage of these content-free dreams was about equal for each of the four suits: 17.6% for Wands, 15.6% for Cups, 12.9% for Swords, and 17.8% for Pentacles.

This method eventually formed the basis for many of my later additions to the Minor Arcana compositions, which were often based on musical, non-textual and non-image-related considerations, but rather upon the musical content of the dream tune (e.g., rhythm, time signature). In some cases, this has resulted in compositions which do not necessarily neatly correspond to the images of the Rider/Waite deck in particular. For example, many of the traditional predictive interpretations of the Swords cards are profoundly negative, but only one of the pieces composed for Swords (the Nine) is in a minor key. I am more confident of the validity of the inner guidance I have received in dreams than in that of the "standard" attributions! Carmen Sorrenti's interpretations of the Sword (Wings) Keys, also derived from her dreams, tend to confirm this, as they are more positive, as shown in Chapter Eleven.

The Minor Arcana compositions tend to be both shorter and less complex than those for the Major Arcana, and – like the zodiacal Keys of the Major Arcana – they are all in only one musical key. This gave me the latitude to choose between 16 and 18 Keys for any one dream tune. For example, a dream tune in C major might be assigned to Key 4, The Emperor, as that represents the Fire sign Aries; or to Key 16, The Tower, because that represents Mars, which is the ruler of Aries; or to Key 19, The Sun or Key 20, Judgment, both of which are associated with the Fire element; or to any of the 14 cards in the suit of Wands. In all cases, most or all of the instruments for which such a piece was scored were in the brass family. The assignments by musical key are given in Figure 5.4 below.

Musical Key	Sign	Major Keys	Minor Keys	Element	Minor Arcana
C	♈	4,16,20	7	Fire	Wands
C#	♉	3,5,21	8	Earth	Pentacles
D	♊	0,1,6	9	Air	Swords
Eb	♋	2,7,12	11	Water	Cups
E	♌	8,19,20	13	Fire	Wands
F	♍	1,9,21	14	Earth	Pentacles
F#	♎	0,1,3,11	15	Air	Swords
G	♏	12,13,16,20	17	Water	Cups
Ab	♐	10,14,20	18	Fire	Wands
A	♑	15,21	4	Earth	Pentacles
Bb	♒	0,1,17	5	Air	Swords
B	♓	2,12,18	6	Water	Cups

Figure 5.4: Musical keys Assigned to Major and Minor Arcana Keys

In a few cases, my original dream attributions to Keys within this range turned out not to fit well musically, and individual themes were then switched from one Key to another within the range of Tarot Keys specified by that key, in order to make more coherent, aesthetically pleasing compositions. This might also entail changing the original time signature from the dream, but *never* the key signature. In the vast majority of cases (96.9%), the music I received in dreams was in a specific time signature, mostly 3/4, 4/4, or 6/8; but in some cases my intuition guided me to use numbers symbolic of the Tarot Key for this purpose; for example, 7/4 for Key 0 because Uranus, its ruler, is associated with the number 7[22]; or 5/4 for Key 5, or 9/8 for Key 9, or 11/4 for Key 11. Sometimes the number of the Key affected the form of the final composition structure as well; for example, Key 7 is set as a theme with seven variations. The distribution of time signatures by suit for the raw tunes is shown in Figure 5.5, though it should be remembered that these may have been changed in the final compositions:

time signature	Major Arcana	Wands	Cups	Swords	Pentacles	Total	%
2/4	5	1	1	3	3	13	1.90%
3/4	42	37	28	29	35	171	25.20%
4/4	110	93	50	73	95	421	62.00%
5/4	1	0	1	0	0	2	0.30%
6/8	25	13	9	9	10	66	9.70%
7/8	1	0	0	0	0	1	0.10%
9/8	4	0	0	0	0	4	0.60%
11/8	1	0	0	0	0	1	0.10%

Figure 5.5: Time Signatures Associated with Tarot Tunes

All of the completed pieces are scored for small instrumental groups, most often of three or four instruments, and never more than nine. There is only one solo piece, the Ten of Pentacles for harp. I originally thought that the Seven of Pentacles was for solo marimba, but I was informed by a marimba player in the Bridgewater Wind Ensemble that it would have to be played by two performers, either on one or two instruments, so it is not really a solo. Most of the pieces are of moderate length, between two and five minutes, and only one (Key 7) is longer than ten minutes. Only two pieces (Key 15 and the Six of Pentacles) are shorter than 2 minutes. The total time length of all 78 compositions is just under 4 3/4 hours – but it is not expected that anyone will play through the entire set at one sitting!

---

[22] See infra, p. 55.

◆ 6 ◆
Methodology

My method for catching dreams -- which I developed while working on the *Gilgamesh Cantata* – is that I give myself a very simple affirmation before going to sleep each night: "I am sleep and I am dream." If I am awakened from a dream in the course of the night – especially if it is a dream which is associated with music – I usually will get out of bed to record it my dream journal. In the case of musical dreams, I will go over the musical selection in my mind several times before doing this, in effect making it an "earworm", and then I will go to the piano to determine on what note the dream music began, and in which key it was. I do not have perfect pitch, but over the course of the project I have become better at accurately identifying the initial note on the piano. Then I transcribe the music into my dream journal in standard musical notation, along with the text of the dream, in longhand[1]. Very often, getting up in the middle of the night to record dreams and then getting back to sleep again resulted in a subsequent recalled dream or dreams. In 105 cases, as shown in Figure 6.1, these re-entries involved additional music, in 53.3% of which I was given a continuation of the same tune:

	reentries	same tune	other
2021	July	0	0
	August	3	2
	September	3	3
	October	7	7
	November	6	6
	December	0	0
2022	January	2	1
	February	4	2
	March	2	1
	April	3	0
	May	3	0
	June	6	9
	July	7	4
	August	1	5
	September	1	1
	October	3	4
	November	2	2
	December	2	2
2023	January	1	0
	total	56	49

Figure 6.1: Dream Reentries with Musical Dream Tarot Themes

---

[1] See Figure 4.4, supra.

A more problematical case was posed by the recall of musical themes which had already been assigned to Keys, but which recurred in subsequent dreams, sometimes in different keys. There have been 29 cases of this, 16 of them in the same key[2], and in all but one case I decided not to reuse the same tune elsewhere. As shown in Figure 6.2, the majority (82.8%) were from the final six months of the project, by which time many tunes had already been assigned to Keys:

Year	Month	Count
2021	July	1
	August	0
	September	0
	October	0
	November	1
	December	1
2022	January	0
	February	1
	March	0
	April	0
	May	0
	June	1
	July	0
	August	2
	September	5
	October	4
	November	3
	December	5
2023	January	5
	total	29

Figure 6.2: Duplicate Tarot Tunes

I have allowed these repetitions to count when considering common dream motifs for the Keys whose tunes they replicate[3], whether or not they are in the same key. But I have no clear idea as to why I was given the same music more than once in dreams. In the very last dream of the project, from January 25, 2023, an explanation for the duplication was given:

> *Someone gives me a tune and asks me to get a blessing for it, to give it more "pizzazz". I enter a Catholic church. Aside from the priest, who stands before the altar with a cup of holy water, I am the only person there. I walk down the aisle to where he is standing and request the blessing. The cup is so full of water that it sloshes over the lip, and some of it lands on the floor before he blesses the tune.*

---

[2] Eight for Wands, seven for Cups, ten for Swords, and three for Pentacles. The one exception was a tune used for both the Three and Four of Wands.

[3] These were used in Chapters 9-12 to determine common themes for each Minor Arcana Key.

The "pizzazz" consisted of adding a run of sixteenth notes to the opening theme for the Queen of Pentacles. The ending of the dream indicated symbolically ("my cup runneth over"[4]) that the rest of the duplicate tune I had been given was . . . superfluous! And perhaps this was also an indication that the entire project was done.

After I awaken in the morning, I transcribe the dream tune or tunes from that night which I previously recorded in my dream journal on the computer, using Finale©[5], a music-writing program, and I enter the dream text into my dream database program. In some cases, I was able to recognize the tune as one already existing in the musical repertoire only after transcribing it in my journal, in which case it was <u>not</u> included in this project, to avoid contamination from day residue.[6] There were altogether 131 cases of this during the project period, 17.1% of all non-Tarot dreams. This is a much higher frequency of non-Tarot-related musical dreams than I experienced before the project, and I expect that this is due to the emphasis on music during this period. All but 23 of these tunes, 82.3%, are by classical composers, as was the case for the music received in dreams prior to the project. Surprisingly, fully 35 of these were by Mozart[7], followed by 9 by Beethoven, 7 by Schubert, 5 by Handel, 4 each by J.S. Bach, Johann Strauss and Tchaikovsky, 3 each by Haydn and Saint-Saens, and 2 each by Holst and Mahler. These ten composers accounted for 73.8% of the classical total. Of the other 29 classical composers whose works I heard in these dreams, none occurred more than once. This differs somewhat from the list of composers whose music I heard prior to the project[8]. Some of these tunes were clearly day residue, in that they were musical pieces I'd heard on the radio shortly before, or pieces which the Wind Band was rehearsing at the time.

The work proceeded at its own pace, with no discernible pattern to the order in which the tunes were given. I scrupulously avoided attempting to force it by asking for the solution to any particular musical problem. Sometimes the choice of which Key to work on was provided by a subsequent dream related to that Key. In general, it has been remarkable how many themes, given seemingly in random order night after night, I was able to fit into each of the final compositions. In many cases, but not always, the fit was very easy. This has convinced me that Whoever is supplying these dreams knows (much better than I ever could) exactly what They are doing!

---

[4] Psalms 23:5

[5] Finale©, DVD version, MakeMusic Inc. My original 2011 version has been upgraded several times.

[6] There are numerous cases throughout the 78 compositions in which short musical phrases were used which may appear in the work of other composers, but this is simply due to the limitations of European musical notation. It was only when <u>whole dream tunes</u> were found to replicate existing works that they were excluded.

[7] Selections from Mozart's *Eine kleine Nachtmusik* appeared several times in dreams. This could have been metaphorical of the project, as most of the tunes I was receiving were indeed "small", in that they were often only a few measures long; and they certainly all were coming at night!

[8] See p. 12, supra.

As an example of how this worked, I had numerous problems with Key 3, The Empress, for which I had an overabundance of themes (31 in all, far more than for any other Key) in three different keys (A, F, and Db major, in association with the Earth element), but I had no clear idea of how to organize them. I had a number of ideas, as well as suggestions from others, about how to resolve this, but I felt it was essential that the solution come from the dreams themselves. Only two weeks before the end of the major reception phase of the project, I had the following pair of dreams on the same night:

> *I and an associate are charged with the task of laying out two adjacent sections of a garden. After a certain amount of working on these sections, they suddenly and unexpectedly merge into a single symmetrical pattern. I see this as either white flowers against a green background or as black musical notes on a white page. This is associated with a tune.*

I commented on this dream, "The tunes I receive for the Musical Dream Tarot do tend to merge unexpectedly together! The tune was in G major (#61), so it goes with Cups."

> *I reenter the preceding dream. The two sections of the garden which my associate and I completed were on the left side. We are now charged with the task of integrating them with the two sections on the right, to make a totally symmetrical pattern around the center. We and the other two people do this by drawing cards from a deck and using their numbers to shift elements around. We are successfully nearing completion of this. A tune plays in the background.*

My comments on this dream were,

> *This counts as a referential dream, since I am indeed using the numbers of the Minor Arcana as means of placing the themes (flowers) into compositions which carry a certain amount of musical symmetry. It gave me, symbolically, the solution to the problem of Key 3: Divide the themes into four groups, and combine them within groups separately before putting all four back together.*[9]

The 31 Key 3 dreams were therefore divided into three groups by key signature, and the dreams in F (the majority of them) were further divided by time signature into two groups – those in duple time and those in triple time – and then the themes within each of the four groups were merged together, polyphonically and/or sequentially, to produce a harmonious and somewhat symmetrical composition. The color green is indeed associated with Key 3.

---

[9] The reference to drawing cards from a deck was the clincher for this association. However, the tune from the first dream was not assigned to Key 3, but remained in G major and was assigned to the Two of Cups.

When I was not sure of which Tarot Key a dream tune went with, I recorded it in Finale© with a notation of what musical key it was in, and I assigned it a sequential number for dreams in that key; as in the example above, "G61"[10]. As noted in Chapter Five, this has particularly been my method when dealing with the Minor Arcana.

In addition to transcribing the music and the dream text, I also have kept careful track of a number of parameters, using two multi-page Excel spreadsheets for this. Keeping careful records has been essential for maintaining order among the abundance of dreams and among all 78 final compositions which comprise this project. The first multi-page spreadsheet, one page of which is shown in Figure 6.3, simply tallies the number of Tarot-related and non-Tarot-related dreams per month[11], as well as the number and Key of the Major Arcana dreams and the number of dreams for each of the suits of the Minor Arcana:

Month:	Major Arcana	Minor-Wands	Minor-Cups	Minor-Swords	Minor-Pentacles	Total Minor Arcana
21-Jun	3	0	0	0	0	0
21-Jul	11	0	1	2	0	3
21-Aug	13	0	0	0	0	0
21-Sep	15	0	0	0	1	1
21-Oct	29	3	1	2	2	8
21-Nov	30	5	3	2	5	15
21-Dec	10	8	12	11	18	49
22-Jan	9	15	8	5	12	40
22-Feb	4	8	8	7	6	29
22-Mar	5	10	4	8	3	25
22-Apr	7	11	5	2	4	22
22-May	8	9	8	8	15	40
22-Jun	7	15	7	15	15	52
22-Jul	8	10	6	12	14	42
22-Aug	7	7	4	12	17	40
22-Sep	5	19	10	6	13	48
22-Oct	9	9	4	14	5	32
22-Nov	9	8	2	7	10	27
22-Dec	6	11	6	9	6	32
23-Jan	1	4	2	1	3	10
total	196	152	91	123	149	515

Figure 6.3: Musical Dream Tarot Dreams per Month Attributed to Major and Minor Arcana

---

[10] In cases where there was a dream reentry on the same or a subsequent night with a tune in the same key and time signature, I counted these as separate dreams but appended an "A" or a "B" (and, in one case, a "C") to the number of the dream.

[11] See Figures 4.2 and 4.3, supra.

Figure 6.4, from another page of this spreadsheet, shows the tallies of the number of dreams of each type (Within Dream, Whole Dream, Hypnopompic, and Referential) per month:

Month	Within Dream	Whole Dream	Hypnopompic	Referential	Inspiration	#
Jun-21	2	1	0	1	0	4
Jul-21	2	8	6	3	1	20
Aug-21	4	5	3	1	1	14
Sep-21	4	11	1	1	0	17
Oct-21	8	7	20	2	0	37
Nov-21	7	12	22	4	0	45
Dec-21	8	12	38	4	0	62
Jan-22	13	8	28	6	0	55
Feb-22	6	5	18	3	1	33
Mar-22	4	6	22	2	0	34
Apr-22	4	3	22	2	1	32
May-22	12	6	29	7	1	55
Jun-22	13	8	38	3	0	62
Jul-22	13	7	29	11	0	60
Aug-22	15	6	25	1	0	47
Sep-22	9	10	34	0	0	53
Oct-22	8	4	30	2	0	44
Nov-22	5	5	26	3	0	39
Dec-22	7	3	28	8	0	46
Jan-23	4	3	6	6	0	19
Total	148	130	425	70	5	778

Figure 6.4: Musical Dream Tarot Dreams by Month by Type of Dream

Figure 6.5, from another page, shows in what order among the dreams of the night the musical dream occurred; a sample month is given below:

August	2022						
rank:	1st	2nd	3rd	4th	5th	6th	Total
of 1	1	X	X	X	X	X	1
of 2	10	7	X	X	X	X	17
of 3	5	1	3	X	X	X	9
of 4	5	2	1	2	X	X	10
of 5	1	0	1	2	1	X	5
of 6	1	1	1	1	0	1	5
Total	23	11	6	5	1	1	47

Figure 6.5: Sample Month's Dreaming by Position of the Tarot Dream in the Night

The second spreadsheet has five pages, one for the Major Arcana and one for each of the Minor Arcana suits, giving the key, the sequential number, the order of appearance among the night's dreaming, the time signature, the number of measures (doubled if the theme is to be repeated), an original expression of the instruments involved, the thematic elements and the emotions associated with the dream text, the total word length of the text, and (once it has been assigned) the final attribution of the theme to a composition. These are organized by final attribution; a sample for the Two of Wands Key is given in Figure 6.6 below:

Key	#	Date	Order	Time Signature	# measures	instruments	dream text elements	emotions	Word Length	Attribution
C	3	11/24/2021	3 of 3	4/4	8	trumpet	balcony,courtyard,large screen TV,wall,eye,news,death,Bill Clinton	shock,sadness	60	2
C	14	12/26/2021	3 of 5	4/4	8	trumpet	sphere,quadrants,red,green,blue,black	none	37	2
C	46A	3/26/2022	2 of 3	4/4	16	horn	newcomer, house, highest point, sunset, horizon	beauty	50	2
C	46B	3/26/2022	3 of 3	3/4	16	horn	group, protest, Gulf Oil, train station, storefronts	anger	64	2
C	53	4/17/2022	1 of 3	4/4	4	trumpet	someone, young women, bare midriff, decency	disapproval	22	2
C	61	5/18/2022	1 of 2	4/4	16	trombone	none	none	4	2
C	65	5/30/2022	2 of 4	4/4	10	trumpet	teenager, mantelpiece, parents' house, sphere,tetrahedron,wood,red	discovery, creative	31	2
C	84	7/14/2022	3 of 5	4/4	8	trombone	young man, young woman, hostage, copper tubing,torture,escape,kindly older man, proof, console, recording, captives, apartment, authorities, arrest	depravity, torture, pleas,help,false claims	167	2
C	127	11/14/2022	1 of 2	4/4	16	trombone	anthropologists, Brazil, tribal cultures, isolated, smile, survival, independence, political influence,bloc,unite	advise, politeness	121	2

Figure 6.6: Sample of Minor Arcana Themes Arranged by Musical Key and Tarot Key

The corresponding page for the Major Arcana is slightly different, in that the dream themes and emotions are not included, because I did not need them to associate the themes with a particular Key beyond their key signature. A sample is shown in Figure 6.7 below:

Key	Musical key	Time Signature	Date	Order	# of measures	instruments	Word Length
0	D	7/8	10/3/2021	1 of 2	17	flute, oboe, clarinet, bassoon	129
0	D	4/4	10/9/2021	1 of 2	9	flute, oboe, clarinet, bassoon	66
0	D	4/4	11/2/2021	2 of 2	8	flute, oboe, clarinet, bassoon	85
0	D	4/4	12/14/2021	3 of 4	16	flute, oboe, clarinet, bassoon	13
1	D	4/4	8/28/2021	1 of 2	16	flute, oboe, english horn, clarinet, bassoon	67
1	D	4/4	8/28/2021	2 of 2	2	flute, oboe, english horn, clarinet, bassoon	50
1	F	4/4	10/22/2021	1 of 2	8	flute, oboe, english horn, clarinet, bassoon	37
1	D	3/4	10/26/2021	1 of 2	16	flute, oboe, english horn, clarinet, bassoon	116
1	F	4/4	11/19/2021	2 of 2	16	flute, oboe, english horn, clarinet, bassoon	170
1	F	4/4	11/22/2021	3 of 3	6	flute, oboe, english horn, clarinet, bassoon	75
1	D	4/4	11/30/2021	3 of 3	3	flute, oboe, english horn, clarinet, bassoon	9
1	D	4/4	5/11/2022	1 of 3	8	chimes	73
1	D	4/4	11/27/2022	1 of 4	8	clarinet	56

Figure 6.7: Sample of Major Arcana Themes Arranged by Musical Key and Tarot Key

Additional pages of this spreadsheet tally the number of themes in each musical key[12]; the number of dream re-entries and whether they contained the same music as the preceding dream[13]; and some statistics on word count which will be presented in Chapter 7.

As shown in Figure 6.8, usually what I hear in the dreams are only 2-bar, 4-bar, 8-bar, or at most 16-bar phrases, which are certainly not complete musical compositions, but which require the use of some compositional skills to transform them into actual pieces:

# of Measures	Major Arcana	Wands	Cups	Swords	Pentacles	Total
1	0	0	0	1	0	1
2	9	2	0	1	1	13
3	7	2	1	3	7	20
4	19	7	6	8	9	49
5	11	1	1	2	0	15
6	14	6	3	4	4	31
7	5	2	0	0	0	7
8	36	41	21	24	37	159
9	2	2	0	2	0	6
10	4	10	3	6	7	30
11	2	0	0	0	0	2
12	8	2	5	8	10	33
13	0	2	2	0	0	4
14	6	1	2	3	1	13
15	2	0	0	0	3	5
16	39	45	27	37	42	190
17	2	1	2	0	0	5
18	5	4	4	3	8	24
19	0	1	0	0	0	1
20	3	5	5	0	5	18
24	2	1	0	1	0	4
25	0	0	0	0	1	1
26	2	0	0	1	0	3
27	0	0	0	1	0	1
28	1	0	2	0	2	5
30	1	1	0	3	1	6
32	4	7	3	5	3	22
34	0	0	0	1	0	1
36	0	0	0	0	1	1
66	0	0	1	0	0	1

Figure 6.8: Number of Measures for Dream Tunes

---

[12] See Figure 5.3.
[13] See Figure 5.4.

In many cases for tunes with even numbers of measures, the total from the dream has been doubled, because in the dream all or part of the tune was repeated. Thus, the totals for 2-, 4-, 8-, and 16-bar phrases combined account for 61.5% of the total.

In almost all cases for this project[14], several dream tunes have gone into the composition of any one completed piece. Welding these tunes into a coherent musical structure involved examining the possibilities for counterpoint, in which different themes are played simultaneously against one another, as well as sequential forms, such as theme and variations and rondo movements, in which one theme is played at the outset, followed by one or more excursions on a second theme, followed by the original theme again: A-B-A or A-B-A-C-A.

While in most cases I have retained the original notes of the dreams when themes are played against one another, in several cases I have felt free to alter a few notes in a line, or even a whole bar or two, to make the themes harmonize. This process also involves scoring accompaniments which harmonize well with the dream tune's theme, and sometimes tossing the theme or fragments of it back and forth among the chosen instruments. As new tunes associated with the Keys were received, they were incorporated by either lengthening the compositions or by substituting them for the non-dream accompaniments, resulting in an increasingly dense polyphonic texture.

The tempo was usually suggested in the dream, but the dynamics, and any accents or slurs which color the original themes, often needed to be added. I also have had to decide on what octave each line of music should be, whether or not to repeat sections of the finished pieces, and in what order to organize the themes. In some cases for the Major Arcana, for reasons explained in Chapter Five[15], there have been some key modulations incorporated into the same piece as well, and these needed to be introduced by transitions. I always play back the music at each point where I have made changes, to make sure that it contains no unintentional discords[16], and I correct these as I find them. Playing the music back also allows me to provide the timing (in minutes and seconds) for each piece, as for example shown in Figure 6.9 below, which also provides the final attribution of each Key, the number of dreams involved, the key and time signature(s), and the instrumentation used:

---

[14] The exception is Key 15, the main theme of which came in a single dream, but there were two inspirational additions to it, as explained in Chapter 7.
[15] See Figure 6.1.
[16] In some cases, intentional discords have been used, for example in Key 13, Death, where they represent the break-up of the crystallized form to release the spirit.

Swords	# dreams	Key	Time Signature (s)	Instrumentation	Timing
A	6	Bb	3/4	flute, oboe, clarinet	3:05
2	7	D	3/4	flute, oboe, clarinet, bassoon	2:40
3	6	Bb	3/4, 4/4, 6/8	flute, clarinet, bassoon, triangle, snare drum	3;20
4	2	Bb	4/4	flute, oboe, clarinet, bassoon	2:33
5	7	D	4/4	flute, oboe, clarinet, bassoon	5:40
6	3	D	3/4, 4/4	flute, clarinet	2:30
7	8	D	3/4, 4/4	flute, oboe, English horn, clarinet, bassoon	4:10
8	4	D	3/4, 4/4	flute, oboe, clarinet, bassoon	2:05
9	4	Bb	4/4	flute, clarinet, bassoon, hand cymbals, bongos	3:15
10	4	D	4/4	flute, oboe, clarinet, English horn, bassoon	4:30
K	3	D	4/4	flute, clarinet, bassoon, snare drum, bass drum	2:25
Q	7	D	4/4, 6/8	flute, clarinet, oboe, bassoon	2:00
N	3	Bb	4/4	flute, clarinet	3:20
P	11	Bb	3/4, 4/4	flute, oboe, clarinet, bassoon	4:15

Figure 6.9: Final Attribution of Dreams to Sword Keys, and Timing of the Pieces

The conclusion of the reception phase of the project was, characteristically, announced by another pair of dreams, on 12/31/2022:

> 1) *I am playing a game of cards with some people. But when my hand is dealt, I suddenly realize that I have no recollection of what the rules of this game are, even though I know that I've played it many times before. This is frustrating!*

> 2) *I am in a large hardware supply store. I have been sent here to obtain a certain mechanical part. I find it; it is a small red and grey metal object. But I suddenly realize that I have no idea of what it does or what it is for, though I know that I knew this when I entered the store. This is frustrating!*[17]

This was, in fact, the day when I finally merged the four sections of the music for Key 3 together. I recorded 34 more dreams with music in them up to January 25th of 2023, but all but seven of these[18] were either previously existing compositions or duplicates of themes I had previously utilized. Another indication of the ending of the reception phase of the project was the observation that any tunes I received in dreams were no longer retained as earworms, as they had been before. Finally, after January 25th there was a gap of over a week before I received any further musical dream themes – and these turned out to be for different compositions – for example, an oboe concerto and music to accompany the Biblical story of Joseph, which I am now in the process of writing.

---

[17] The second dream contains some day residue, as I had visited a hardware supply store the day before.
[18] One Major Arcana, three Wands, one Cup, and two Pentacles.

◆ 7 ◆
Results of the Project

With only a few exceptions which I will describe shortly, all of the musical themes used for the Musical Dream Tarot compositions derived directly from my dreams. Concentration on this project certainly increased my dream recall frequency overall, from 1.5 per night to over 3.0 per night during the peak periods[1], with a total of 1512 dreams in all, 778 of them (50.4% of the total) related to the project[2]. As Figure 7.1 below shows, the peak for dreams for the Major Arcana was earlier in the process, in October and November of 2021, with a high of 30 dreams in November, after which it declined to ten or fewer dreams per month. The peaks for dreams involving the Minor Arcana were in December of 2021 and in June and September of 2022, with a high of 51 dreams in June. No doubt the June peak was due to my preparation for giving a 90-minute presentation on the project at the 2022 IASD conference in July.

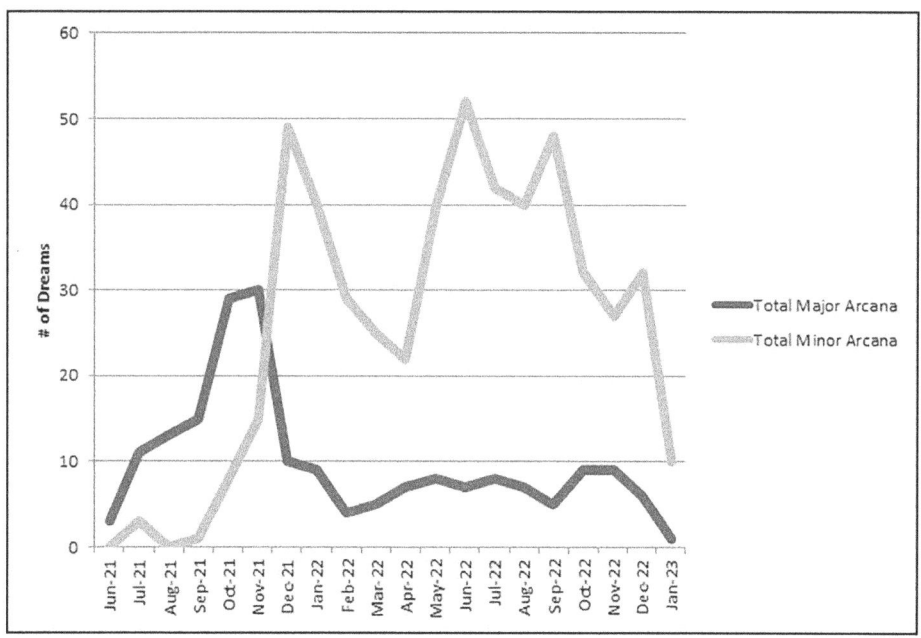

Figure 7.1: Frequencies of Major and Minor Arcana Dreams by Month

The most frequent type of Musical Dream Tarot dream, somewhat more than half (425, 54.5%), was of tunes received in the hypnopompic state. As noted in Chapter Three, this is a stage in

---

[1] The average number of recalled dreams per night during the entire period was 2.57.
[2] Subsequent to the conclusion of the reception phase of the project, my dream recall frequency briefly returned to a more normal rate, but increased again as I began to receive tunes for new compositions.

which the dreamer is coming out of the sleep state. My practice while in this liminal state is to lie very still without changing my sleep position as I go over the content of the dream, and a tune will often emerge at the end of this recollection. My sleep state for these musical selections could be considered as semi-lucid in nature, as the tune was a continuation of the dream while I was aware of having dreamt. A much smaller number (148, 19.0%) were tunes embedded within the content of the dream, and there were also a slightly smaller number (130, 16.7%) in which all that I recalled of the dream was the tune itself. As I noted in Chapter Three, it is possible that I simply didn't recall the contents of some of the dreams of the latter type. A relatively small number of dreams (70, 9.0%) did not contain any actual music, but simply referred to the project itself or provided guidance as to how to execute it.

A very small number of selections (7, 0.9%) were the result of meditative states, intuitive inspirations, or synchronicities I recognized subsequent to dreaming. These are noted in the "inspiration" column of Figure 6.4 above. These all included already existing music: the incorporation of the Dies Irae theme into the music for Key 15, The Devil; the use of the Renaissance tune "La Folia" in the excursions for Key 0, The Fool[3]; Georg Friedrich Handel's "See, the Conquering Hero Comes" from his oratorio *Judas Maccabaeus*[4] as the basis for the set of seven variations for Key 7, The Chariot; the use of themes from Richard Wagner's *Tristan und Isolde*[5] for Key 6, The Lovers; from the Renaissance dance tune "Laura Suave" by Fabritio Caroso for Key 2, The High Priestess[6]; and from Josquin des Pres' fanfare tune "Vive le Roi"[7] for Key 4, The Emperor. Key 15 also includes a tune from Stephen Schwartz's *Godspell*.[8] With the exception of the last, all of these tunes are in the public domain.

The frequencies of these five types of sources are also shown in Figure 7.2, opposite. A comparison with Figure 3.2 for the Gilgamesh Cantata dreams will show that the hypnopompic dreams were far more frequent in the Musical Dream Tarot project, and that the referential dreams were much less frequent than they were in the earlier project. The percentages of tunes embedded within dreams, and of dreams in which the music was the only recalled feature, were about the same for both projects. I speculated that the incidence of referential dreams might increase subsequent to the completion of the project, as was the case for the Gilgamesh Cantata – but even when those

---

[3] Many composers have written variations on these two anonymous themes.
[4] Georg Frederic Handel,"See, the Conquering Hero Comes!" from *Judas Maccabeus*. https://www.youtube.com/watch?v=8p1BedwyFKY. The Key portrays a conquering warrior.
[5] Richard Wagner, *Tristan und Isolde*. https://www.youtube.com/watch?v=IdjFBW-S3z0.
[6] Fabritio Caroso, "Laura Suave". https://sonichits.com/video/Fabritio_Caroso/Laura_Suave?track=1
[7] Josquin des Pres, "Vive le Roi". https://www.youtube.com/watch?v=Z3rpUscM9KQ.
[8] Stephen Schwartz, "Prepare Ye the Way of the Lord", from *Godspell*. https://www.youtube.com/watch?v=c1SiaCV26aQ.

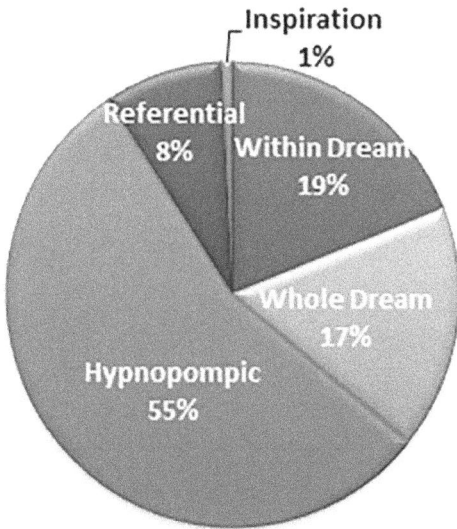

Figure 7.2: Distribution of Musical Dream Tarot Dreams by Type of Dream

were subtracted from the total for the earlier project[9], the percentage of hypnopompic dreams did not rise above 18%. However, this did not occur, and as noted in Chapter Six, after about a week's lapse I began receiving music in dreams for other compositions. There have been a few subsequent dreams which referenced the project, but they did not include any significant information. In addition, in about a quarter of the dreams which provided music for the cantata I saw the notes on a musical staff or score. This has been a very rare occurrence for the Musical Dream Tarot, with only thirteen instances. I currently have no explanation for these differences.

Ever since the early sleep laboratory studies of the 1950s, it has been established that dreams are most likely to occur in REM (rapid-eye-movement) sleep periods, of which there are normally five per night for most people; and also that the duration of these periods tends to increase over the course of the night.[10] While subsequent researchers have established that dreaming can also take place during non-REM sleep[11], REM sleep remains the most studied sleep stage for dream research. In no nights during this period did I recall more than six dreams. Six-dream nights were very infrequent (1.4% of the total) and did not commence until August of 2022. However, nights on which I recorded five dreams were more than five times as frequent as six-dream nights, at 7.2%, and were actually more than twice as frequent as nights on which I recorded only one dream (3.2%). The number of nights per month in which I recalled only one dream tended to decline over the course of the project, as shown in Figure 7.3. Nights with three recorded dreams were the

---

[9] See Figure 6.4.
[10] Eugene Aserinsky and Nathaniel Kleitman, Regularly Occurring Periods of Eye Motility, and Concomitant Phenomena during Sleep. *Science.* 1953:118:273–4.
[11] Mark Solms, The Interpretation of Dreams and the Neurosciences. In *Freud's Traumdeuting.* Fischer Verlag, Frankfurt am Main, 1999.

most frequent, at 39.0%, followed by nights with two recorded dreams (27.2%) and four recorded dreams (22.1%). As shown in Figure 7.4, the trend line slopes for nights with three, four, and five recalled dreams increased similarly over the period of the project, while those with two recalled dreams had a relatively flat trend line.

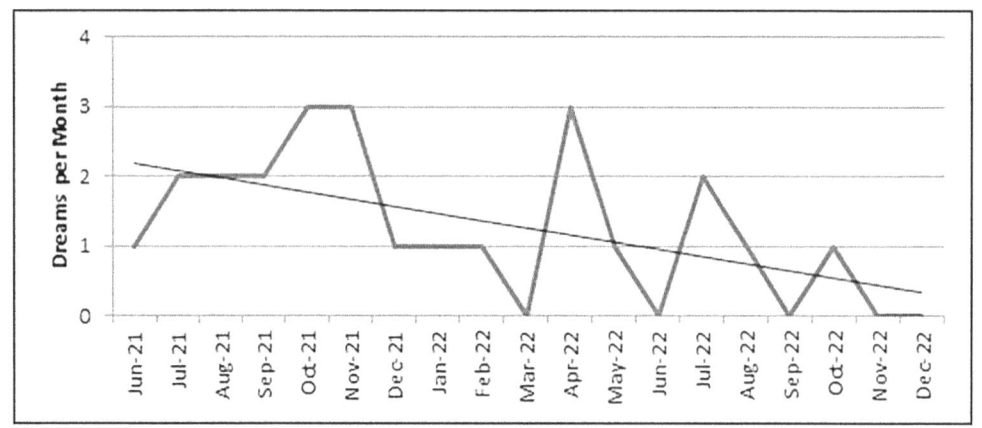

Figure 7.3: Number of Nights with Only One Recalled Dream, by Month

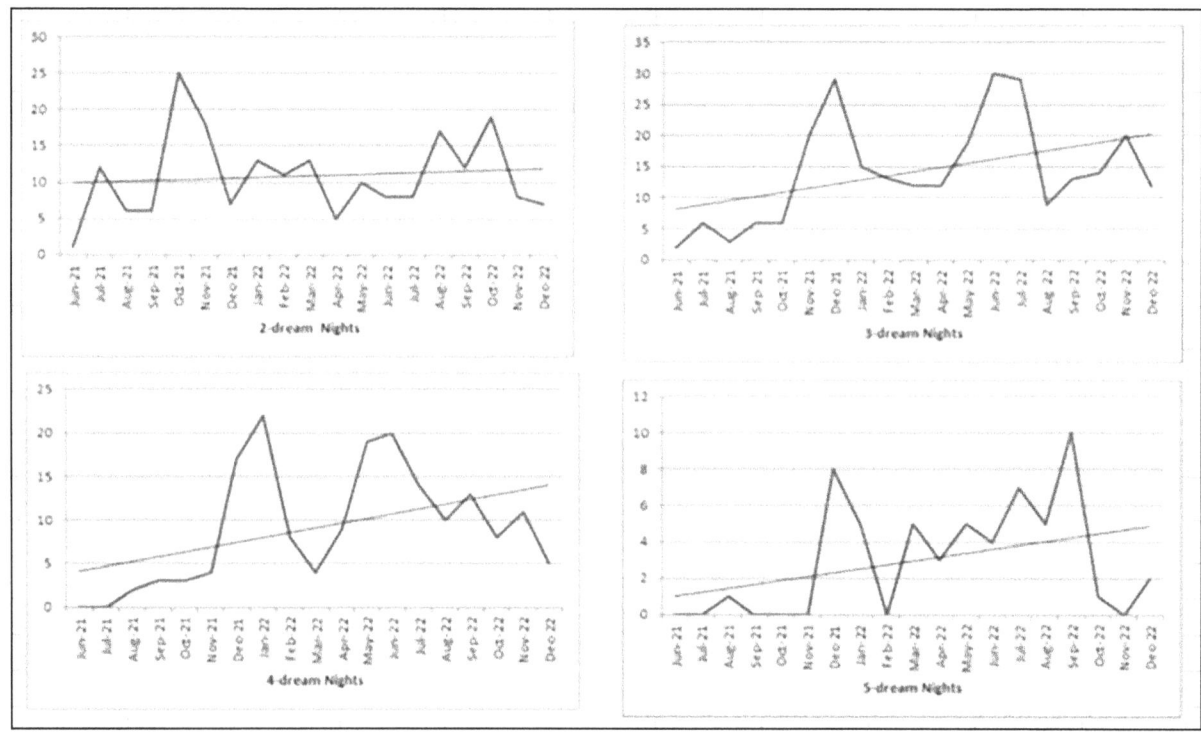

Figure 7.4: Number of Nights with 2, 3, 4, or 5 Recalled Dreams, by Month

As shown in Figure 7.5, all four dream types tended to occur most frequently as the first dream of the night, though this was slightly exaggerated for tunes embedded within dreams and whole dreams. Whole dreams were much less frequent as second dreams, though the other three types had similar frequencies. For third dreams, the embedded dreams were less frequent, with the other three types about equal. Whole dreams were the most frequent in fourth position, while referential dreams were most frequent in fifth position. Sixth position dreams were so infrequent that they were not included in this figure.

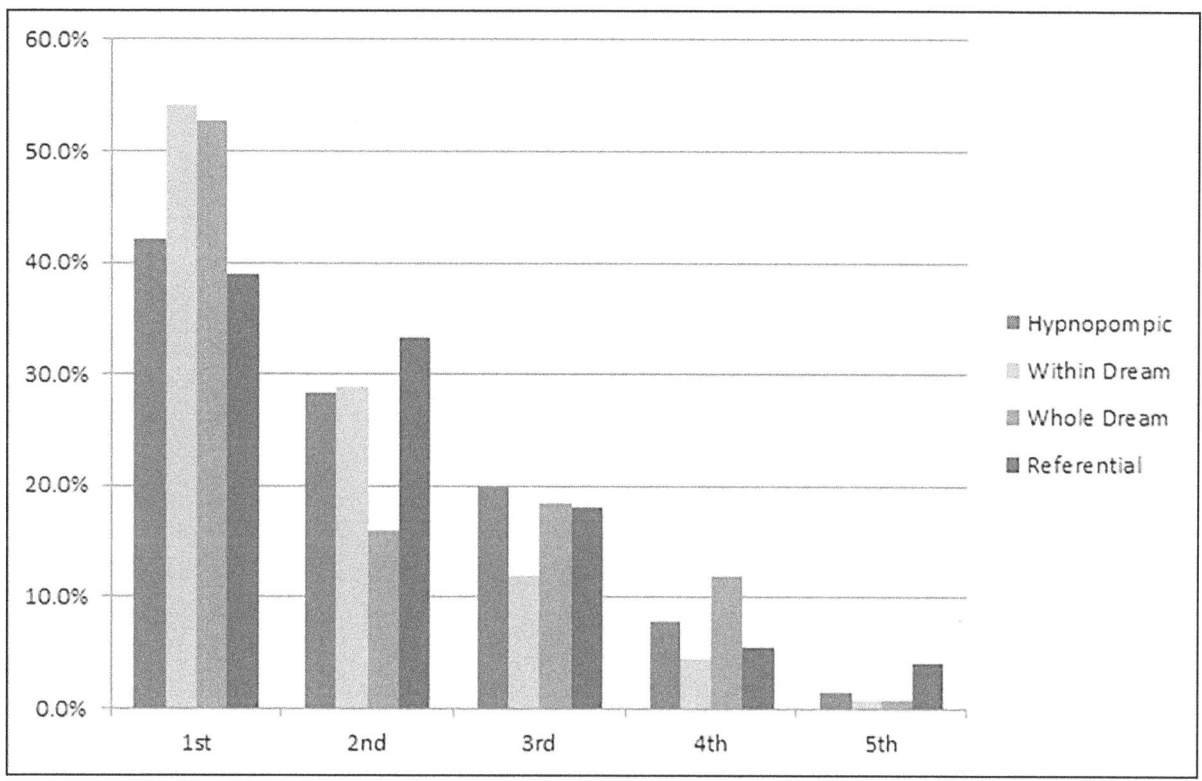

Figure 7.5: Average Position of Tarot Dreams within the Night's Dreaming

None of my dreaming during this period took place in a sleep lab, so I have no direct quantitative data on how long any of my sleep stages were. However, I have taken the length of the dream texts as a kind of proxy for dream length, which is why word count was a parameter I collected for each of the Musical Dream Tarot dreams.[12] There were some significant differences among these types of dreams as to the number of words their texts contained and in what order they tended to occur in the night's dreaming. As shown in Figure 7.6 below, the hypnopompic dreams

---

[12] Some of the methodology described here was developed for a study of my dreams about an archaeological site: Curtiss Hoffman, Dreaming in the Digging Fields, *International Journal of Dream Research* 14(2), 2021. https://journals.ub.uniheidelberg.de/ index.php/IJoDR/article/view/76699.

tended to be the longest, with an average of 114 words and a range from 12 to 526 words. Tunes embedded within dream texts and dreams without music which only referenced the project had about equal average word lengths, 82 and 84 words respectively, with ranges for embedded dreams from 7 to 630 words and for referential dreams from 12 to 431 words. Dreams which consisted of only a tune were radically different in length from the other types, with an average word length of only 8 words and a range from 4 to 56 words. The text of the shortest of these dreams, of which there were 76 examples, was simply, "I hear a tune," while the longer dream texts provided some description of the tune itself.

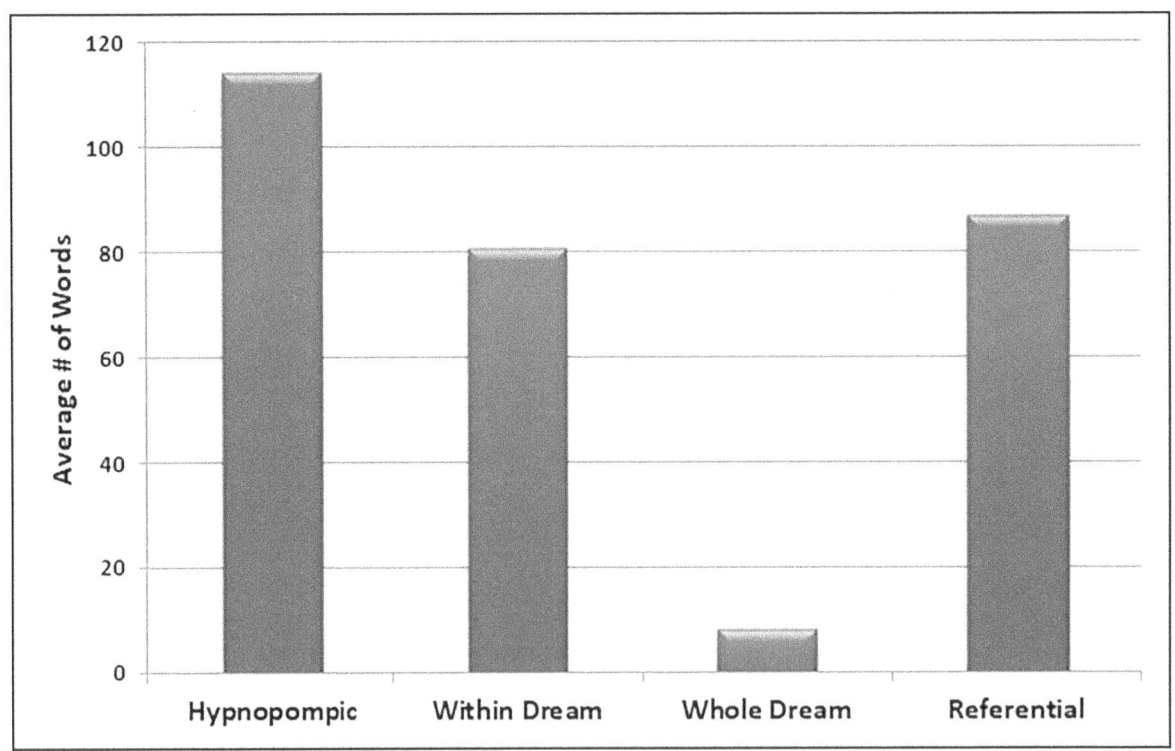

Figure 7.6: Word Count Averages for Musical Dream Tarot Dream Types

As shown in Figure 7.7 below, hypnopompic dreams were most often the wordiest (longest?) dream type in most positions during the night, and were the only ones to appear as the sixth dream of the night. They were exceeded in average word count by embedded dreams at the fourth position and by referential dreams at the fifth position. The average word length for embedded dreams was close to equal to that of the hypnopompic dreams at positions two and three. Whole dreams had a uniformly low word count at positions one through four, and did not occur at positions five and six.

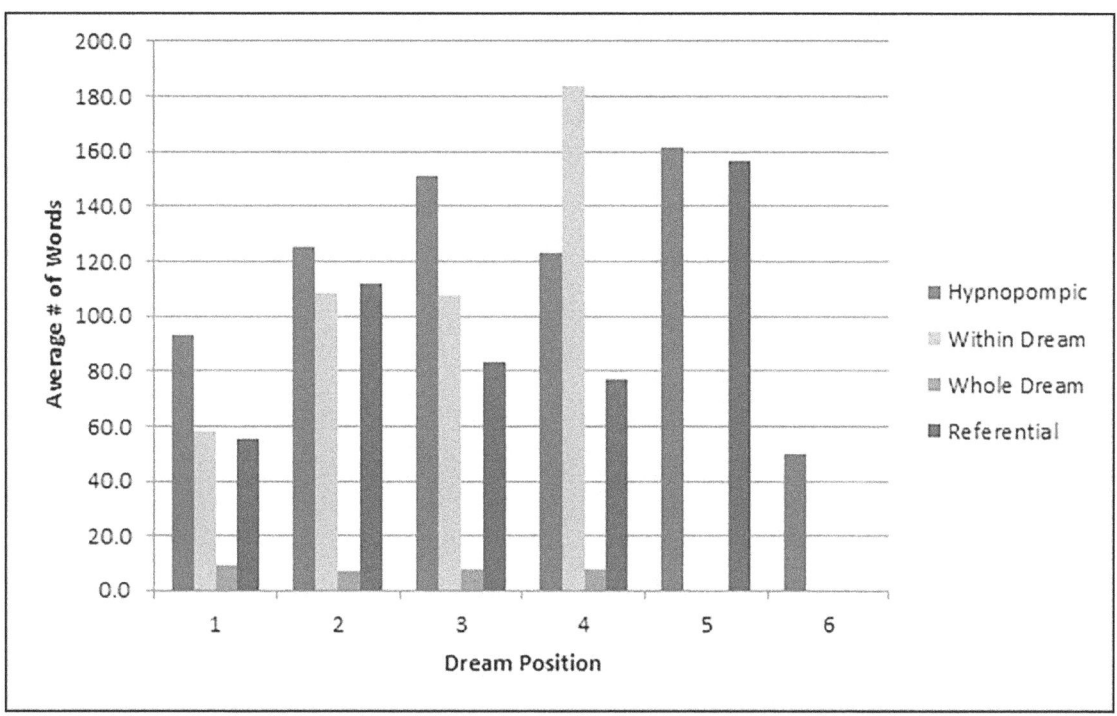

Figure 7.7: Average Word Counts by Dream Position for Dream Types

For all Tarot dreams combined, Figure 7.8 shows that while first dreams tended to be shorter, dream texts in positions two through four were almost exactly equal in length, while only those in position five tended to be much longer. The number of dreams in position six was so small that the decline shown there may not be a significant result. However, this does not take into account the fact that on more than 2/3 of the nights during the project I recalled no more than three dreams.

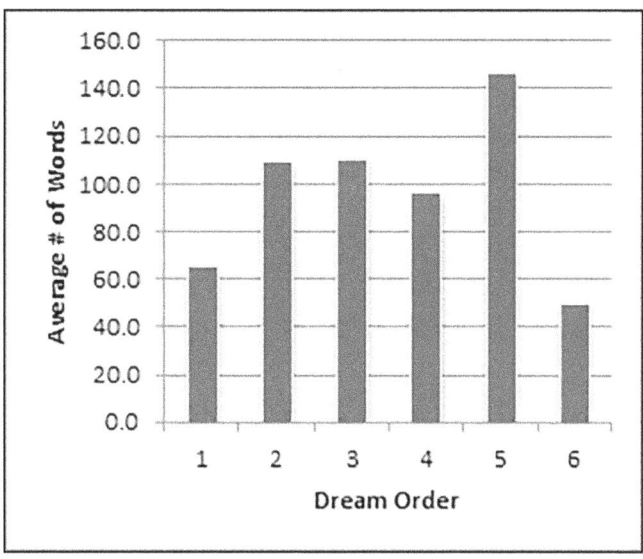

Figure 7.8: Average Word Count by Position for All Tarot Dreams

Another way of measuring this is to look at the distribution of text length by dream type for the first dream of the night, the last dream of the night, and a combination of all dreams from the middle of the night. I did not record the time at which I awakened from any of these dreams, but at least I can specify which dreams were first, medial, and last in a night. The results are shown in Figure 7.9, again by dream type:

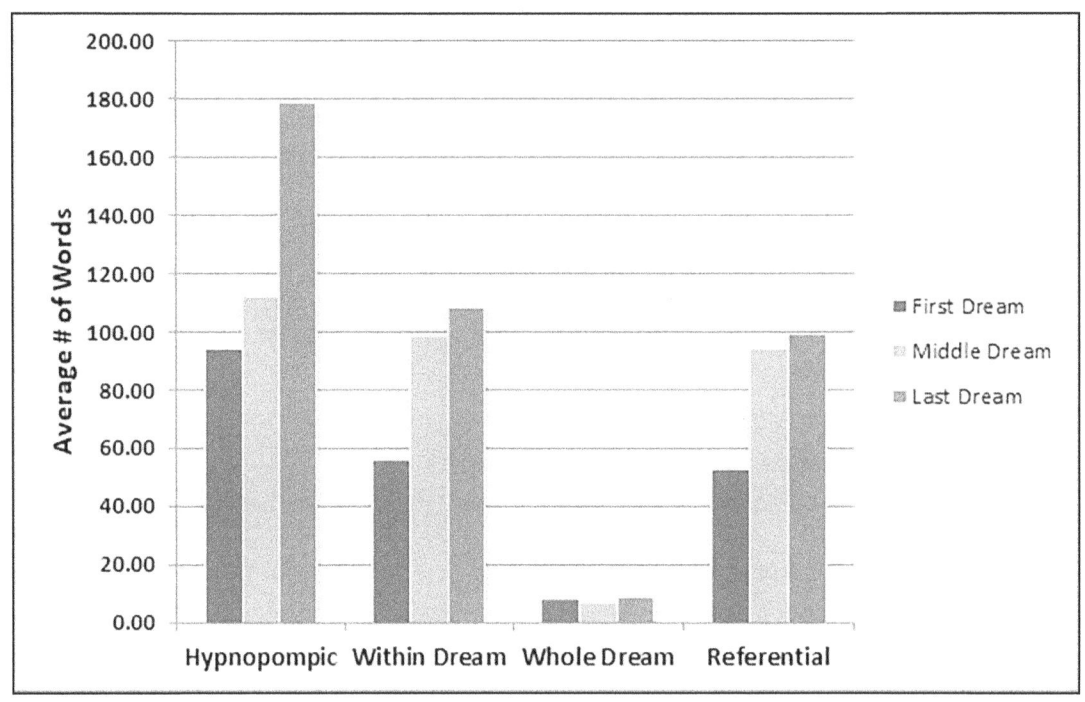

Figure 7.9: Average Word Count by Dream Type for First, Middle, and Last Tarot Dreams

The results are potentially challenging to the dream theory prediction that REM periods tend to increase through the course of a night's dreaming. For hypnopompic dreams, by far the largest number, the medial dreams had only slightly longer average word lengths than the initial dreams, though the texts of the last dreams were certainly much longer, slightly less than twice as long as the initial dreams on average. For tunes embedded within dreams and for referential dreams, the initial dream text lengths were much shorter, but medial dreams were only slightly shorter than final dreams. Whole dreams had nearly equal average low word counts whenever they occurred during the night, though final dreams were very slightly longer in average word count. I will leave it to the quantitative dream researchers to figure out whether this is a significant challenge to dream theory!

An issue which was raised by some IASD conference attendees who were present at my talk at the 2022 conference is what to do when Tarot cards are drawn "reversed" – that is, upside down. I considered a number of options for this; for example, actually writing the music backwards, or in harmonic inversion, or in minor for major keys and in major for minor keys. I actually tried some of these out – for example, scoring the music for Key 12, The Hanged Man as a "crab canon", in which the notes are played forwards from the start to a midpoint and backwards from the end to the same midpoint. This did not work well from a musical perspective. I also tried to rewrite the music for the Nine of Wands, which is in G minor, in its relative major, Bb – but that also did not convey the emotional content of the music well. Ultimately, I decided not to double my workload by adding "reversed" versions of the Keys.

What follows in the next five chapters are descriptions of each of the 78 musical pieces which accompany the Tarot Keys, along with both the traditional (e.g. the Rider/Waite deck[13] and the Paul Foster Case deck[14]) and Carmen Sorrenti's Pholarcos deck's statements about the significance of each Key[15]; accompanied by statements from *Sefer Yetzirah*[16], *The Rays and the Initiations*[17], and *Esoteric Astrology*[18] by Alice Bailey for the Major Arcana; some of P.D. Ouspensky's meditations on the Major Arcana[19], as well as my own impressions, based upon my Tarot notebook, for the Major Arcana; and my dream texts for the Minor Arcana.[20] The thumbnail descriptions of the Major Arcana Keys are taken from the Case deck and the Pholarcos deck, while those for the Minor Arcana are taken from the Rider/Waite deck and the Pholarcos deck[21]. The latter are highly divergent in almost all cases[22]. I can affirm from experience that the Case and Sorrenti Major Arcana function as doorways into other realms of consciousness, but as I observed in Chapter One, the Waite Minor Arcana images seem more prosaic and do not have the resonance for me that the Case and Pholarcos Major Arcana and the Pholarcos Minor Arcana have.

---

[13] Waite, op.cit.

[14] Case, op.cit., pp. 213-216.

[15] Sorrenti, op.cit. As noted above, Sorrenti uses alternatives to the traditional suits: Sparks (Wands), Coral (Cups), Wings (Swords), and Spirals (Pentacles).

[16] Ariyeh, op. cit. Each Hebrew letter referenced in this work corresponds to one of the Major Arcana.

[17] Alice A. Bailey, *The Rays and the Initiations*. Lucis Publishing, New York, 1960.

[18] Alice A. Bailey, *Esoteric Astrology*. Lucis Publishing, New York, 1951.

[19] Ouspensky, op.cit., pp. 202-215. I have not used some with whose content I disagree.

[20] "Common" themes and emotions are defined as those which occurred more than once in association with the tunes for any particular Key. The number in parentheses after the theme or emotion denotes the number of times it occurred in the dreams for that Key. This may indicate the strength of that theme or emotion.

[21] These are taken from the booklet accompanying the deck and Carmen Sorrenti's web-based book, *The Pholarcos Tarot: A Pack of Alchemical Companions*. https://www.carmensorrenti.com/services-nueva, 2022.

[22] Only three of the 56 Minor Arcana have common themes in the two decks: the Six of Wands (a mounted horseman), the Four of Cups (a man sitting beneath a tree), and the Seven of Cups (chalices).

Carmen Sorrenti commented to me about the process by which she transformed her dream images into Keys,

> "As a general reflection, it was an ongoing dialogue between the dreams, the essential meaning of each card, the Pholarchos as guides and the creative/visionary state of mind. I did not have a systematic method aside from tuning deeply into each card with my intent and trusting the process. I find this makes synchronicities light up and lead the way—you just know when the card has hit the 'right note' so to speak. I was immersed in it so it became an all-consuming language. I noticed that being in touch, vividly in touch with my inner child was a key component. The inner child seems to always know how to follow the creative wisdom that is wanting to come through."[23]

This is actually very comparable to my own process of assigning tunes to Keys, as documented in Chapter Five. The music felt intuitively right to me for the Keys for which it was selected in every case. Readers are encouraged to reach their own intuitive conclusions, based upon the feelings evoked by the music.

---

[23] Carmen Sorrenti, personal communication, 2/4/2023.

◆ 8 ◆
The Major Arcana

In all, there were 185 dreams associated with the Major Arcana, in all twelve keys of the diatonic scale. Altogether, the 22 Major Arcana pieces are 1 hour, 41:35 minutes in length.

Key 0 – The Fool

In the Case deck, the androgynous Fool, in motley, accompanied by her/his little dog, appears about to plunge off a mountainous precipice – but if one looks carefully, one can see that his/her feet are not actually touching the ground! There are ten wheels, representing the ten Sephiroth, on his/her garment or chest. Waite associates this card with "folly, mania, extravagance, intoxication, delirium, frenzy, bewrayment." Case has "in spiritual matters: originality, audacity, venturesome quest. In material matters: folly, eccentricity, inconsiderate action." Ouspensky says. "The four magic symbols, the wand, the cup, the sword and the pentacle. The fool always carries them with him, but he does not understand what they mean. Do you not see that it is you, yourself?" In the Pholarcos deck, The Fool is shown as an androgyne in blue, with a pair of triangles at her/his brow and ten circles (representing planets) on his/her chest: "a heart connection to the movements of creation." Sorrenti states further, "the vital force whose knowledge is unsurpassed takes you through the varied inns of consciousness, this your pilgrimage to life. Where will vision and swift feet take you?" Key 0 is attributed to the Air element, and also to the planet Uranus. In *Esoteric Astrology*, Uranus is associated with the Seventh Ray of Ceremonial Order[1], which is becoming more prominent nowadays as the Sun at Spring Equinox is seen rising in the sign of Aquarius, of which Uranus is the exoteric ruler. The affirmation for the Seventh Ray is "The highest and the lowest meet."[2] This Key is associated with the Hebrew letter Aleph, the Ox, which in the Sefer Yetzirah is attributed to the Fiery or Scintillating Intelligence. I think of The Fool as representing that which is unmanifest but which underlies all manifestation, the cosmic seed from which all existence continually springs, which transcends all dualities, including the duality of existence and non-existence. A passage in Psalm 14 states, "The Fool hath said in his heart, there is no God."[3] But the word for "there is no", in Hebrew "Ain"[4], is an anagram for "Ani", "I am", so on one level the Tarot Fool, as the Unmanifest, is saying "I am God". Moreover, in Qabbalah the word "Ain"

---

[1] Alice A. Bailey, 1951, op. cit., pp. 200-201. For this project, I have used the exoteric rulers of the signs as traditionally given in astrological texts. The Tibetan provides an entirely different set of esoteric rulers in this volume which I have not used.
[2] Ibid., 1960, p. 518.
[3] Psalms 14:1.
[4] Not to be confused with 'Ayin, the letter associated with Key 15, The Devil, which uses a different initial consonant absent from English.

has a specialized meaning; it refers to a level beyond the highest level of the Tree of Life[5], so from this perspective the statement could be interpreted "Nothing (= 0) is God." There is definitely something playfully Tricksterish about this figure![6] It is as if the Unmanifest is playing a vast and incomprehensible joke on all that It creates, for Its own amusement.

The piece is scored for woodwind quartet (flute, oboe, clarinet, and bassoon) and is entirely in the key of D major. It is a Vivace rondo, A:B:A:C:A:D:A, in which the rondo theme, taken up by each of the instruments in turn, is in the unusual time signature of 7/4, which imparts a sense of precarious imbalance to the piece. This is emphasized in the last two repetitions of the rondo by the insertion of seemingly random notes beneath the melodic line. The three excursions from the rondo theme have a persistent thematic motif, "La Folia", a tune derived from Renaissance music, which was an inspirational incorporation. This motif becomes increasingly pronounced from one excursion to the next. The first excursion is in 6/8 time; the second and third in 4/4 time. Altogether, this piece is made up of four dream segments, and is 5:00 minutes long.

Key 1 – The Magician

In the Case deck, The Magician, in a white robe, stands with his wand upraised within a garden of roses and lilies, about to manifest his desire, while the symbols of the four elements/suits – his "elemental weapons" – are on an altar table beside him. An infinity sign hovers over his head. Waite associates this card with "skill, diplomacy, address, sickness, pain, loss, disaster, self-confidence, will." Case has "constructive power, initiative, skill, subtle craft, occult wisdom and power." Ouspensky says, "His hands flitted about swiftly as though playing with the four signs of the elements, and I felt that he held some mysterious threads which connected the earth with the distant luminaries." In the Pholarcos deck, a two-headed magician, male to the left and female to the right, oversees the magical work. The man has cultivated a wolf howling at the Moon in his chalice, while the woman has cultivated a dragon under the Sun in hers. A Tricksterish male figure to the left of the man drops spheres with symbols for Mercury, Jupiter, Neptune, and Pluto; while a bird to the woman's right lays eggs representing the four elements. Below, the symbols of the zodiacal signs are engraved on the edge of an altar table. Sorrenti states, "the sky measures time that we may know what is ripe and what is moving – stones, waves, roots will do the same

---

[5] It is the first of three "veils of negative existence": Ain (Nothing), Ain Soph (Terminal Nothing), and Ain Soph Aur (Terminal Illuminated Nothing). https://modernphilosophystandards.com/2-the-universe/the-kabbalah-ain-soph-aur-and-heavenly-father/.

[6] This is doubtless the reason that, in certain card games, a winning combination is referred to as a "trick", or a "trump"; and the Joker (Fool), when used, is the highest trump of them all, and is a "wild" card. The word "trump" (> French *trompe*, trick, as in *trompe l'oeil*) is sometimes used to describe the Tarot Keys.

if you can perceive the echo." Key 1 is attributed to the Air element, through its association with the planet Mercury, which is the ruler of the Air sign of Gemini, associated with D major. Mercury expressses the Fourth Ray of Harmony through Conflict, for which the Word of Power is "Two merge with one."[7] Mercury also is the ruler of the Earth sign of Virgo, associated with F major. This Key is associated with the Hebrew letter Beth, the House, which in the Sefer Yetzirah is attributed to the Intelligence of Transparency, and to the qualities of life and death. On the Qabbalistic Tree of Life, Mercury is associated with Splendor (Hod). In the system of the chakras I learned In SOTGO, Mercury is related to the Throat center – the place for the utterance of magical formulas. The Magician is the epitome of one-pointed concentration, or Will, which is the necessary prerequisite for all manifestation[8]. Will is the chief attribute of the First Ray, which is associated with both the destruction of the old forms and the initiation of the new.[9] By separating the polarities joined in the androgynous (Key 0) universe, he brings about manifestation on the physical plane, and the form which he has in his mind is crystallized. For a brief moment in time, he releases that which is eternally joined in the Unmanifest, and manifestation results.

The piece begins with an Allegro introduction in 4/4 time in F major, but it transitions to 3/4 time in D major. It returns to 4/4 time but remains in D major to the end. It is scored for woodwind quintet (the quartet plus English horn), accompanied by timpani and chimes. It is made up of nine dream segments, and is 6:15 minutes long.

Key 2 – The High Priestess

In the Case deck, The High Priestess is enthroned before a veil displaying palms (male) and pomegranates (female), behind which is the Sea. She sits between the pillars of Solomon's Temple: Yakin (Right) and Bo'az (Might). She holds in her hand the scroll of the Torah, and the bottom of her blue robe morphs into flowing water. Waite associates this card with "secrets, mystery, the future as yet unrevealed . . . silence, tenacity, wisdom, science." Case has "all meanings derivable from duality. Fluctuation, reaction, secrets, things hidden, unrevealed future." Ouspensky says, "In order to enter the temple it is necessary to lift the second veil and pass between the two columns. And in order to pass between them it is necessary to obtain possession of the keys, to read the book and understand the symbols. The knowledge of good and evil awaits you." In the Pholarcos deck, the virginal oracular priestess has hair of flame, and there is an open eye in the vegetation below. Sorrenti states, "The sage she communes with burns away all veils, rapture palpable through the smoke. A ship set sail on the sea of dreaming, so that all may live." Key 2 is attributed to the Moon and to the Water element, the three signs for which are Cancer (Eb major),

---

[7] Alice Bailey, 1960, loc.cit.
[8] Alice Bailey, *From Intellect to Intuition*. Lucis Publishing, New York, 1932. pp. 98-99.
[9] Alice Bailey, *Esoteric Psychology,* v. 1. Lucis Publishing, New York, 1936. pp, 415-416.

Scorpio (G major), and Pisces (B major). This Key is associated with the Hebrew letter Gimel, the Camel, which in the Sefer Yetzirah is attributed to the Uniting Intelligence, and to the qualities of peace and strife. The Moon in the Tibetan's writings veils Neptune, which expresses the Sixth Ray of Devotion and Idealism. The Word of Power for this Ray is "The highest light controls."[10] On the Qabbalistic Tree of Life, the Moon is associated with Foundation (Yesod). In the system of the chakras I learned In SOTGO, the Moon is related to the Ajna center above the eyes, the so-called Third Eye. The Moon governs the tides and the cycles, and in one sense all of the water which flows through the Tarot derives from her robe. The High Priestess is at the margin between the sea and the land, and her veil conceals that which is not yet manifest. On the Tree of Life, the two pillars between which she sits represent Severity (the left-hand path) and Mercy (the right-hand path); hence, she is in the position of the middle path, Mildness. She is ever virgin. She represents the function of memory; the record of all past events is contained in her scroll. Memory is closely related to the unconscious mind. An affirmation of the relationship between her and the Magician: "My unconscious is a clear reflecting instrument with which I can hear below the reflection of the Voice from above. Responding to the instructions of the Voice, I take control over the forces of my personality." In other words, the Magician, as Mercury the Lord of Language, must learn the tongue of the unconscious in order to converse with the High Priestess.

The opening theme is an Andantino in 3/4 time in B major, but it transitions to G major, and later to 6/8 time. Near the end there is a further transition to 4/4 time and Eb major. The piece is scored for string quartet (2 violins, viola, and cello) plus a triangle, is comprised of 7 dream segments, and is 4:35 minutes long.

Key 3 – The Empress

In the Case deck, The Empress, in green, obviously pregnant, sits on a bench in a field of ripe wheat, her foot on a crescent Moon, holding a heart-shaped copper shield with a dove on it. Waite associates this card with "fruitfulness, initiative, action, long days, clandestine, the unknown, difficulty, doubt, ignorance." Case has "fruitfulness, beauty, luxury, pleasure, success." Ouspensky queries her, "why is everything so radiant and joyful and happy around you? Do you not know that there is the grey, weary autumn, the cold, white winter? Do you not know that there is death, black graves, cold damp sepulchers, cemeteries?" Her reply is to smile at him, "and beneath her smile I suddenly felt that in my soul the flower of some bright understanding was opening, as if something was being revealed to me, and the terror of death began to depart from me." In the Pholarcos deck, the bare-breasted Empress, "the earth personified", is surrounded by vegetation, with a spray of five roses from her heart to her throat, while the crescent Moon is behind her; a blue bird perches on its lower horn. Sorrenti states, "The Earth constantly gives birth, every mol-

---

[10] Bailey, 1960, loc.cit.

ecule a ladybug spinning ecstasy . . . for each wave of becoming there is a mystery of origin." Key 3 is attributed to Venus and to the Earth element, the three signs for which are Taurus (Db major), Virgo (F major), and Capricorn (A major). In addition, Venus is the ruler of Taurus. Venus expresses the Fifth Ray of Concrete Mind, for which the Word of Power is "Three minds unite."[11] This Key is associated with the Hebrew letter Daleth, the Door, which in the Sefer Yetzirah is attributed to the Luminous Intelligence, and to the qualities of wisdom and folly. On the Qabbalistic Tree of Life, Venus is associated with Victory (Netzach). In the system of the chakras I learned in SOTGO, Venus is related to the heart center. The Empress is the door through which all Life emerges; she bears within her womb the seeds of all that exist, similar to Noah's ark. The dove which flies from her shield is the purified, oxygenated blood nourishing all the cells. The dove (Hebrew Yonah) is the prophet Jonah who was swallowed by the big fish (womb) and emerged after three days to preach to the people of Nineveh, the shrine of the Fish-goddess (Ninua). The dove also brought the tidings of land to Noah. Doves in Graeco-Roman religion were sacred to Aphrodite/Venus.[12] The Empress is the nourisher of form and of the evolution of form, which takes place in all its cycles in every corner of the universe. No place exists that is not involved in the forward progress of matter and of spirit, and no place may be found that does not fit into some phase of her law.

The piece is scored for a trio of vibraphone, marimba, and piano. It is constituted of five highly polyphonic sections, the last being a reprise of the first. It begins, Andante, with a flowing tune in 3/4 time in Db major, leading into a 4/4 section in the same key. This modulates into a 6/8 section in A major, which in turn morphs into a 6/8 section in F major, followed by a 4/4 section in that key. Each of these sections features multiple themes played polyphonically against one another on various of the instruments. The piece concludes with a reprise of the opening music in Db major. It is comprised of 31 dream segments, the most by far of any of the Keys, and is 5:10 minutes long. Due to its complexity, it was the last of the Keys to be completed.

Key 4 – The Emperor

In the Case deck, The Emperor, in steel armor, sits enthroned upon a cube in a red mountainous area, holding the orb and scepter of his office. His legs are crossed and his arms form a triangle – combined, they form the alchemical symbol for Sulphur, the invigorating male essence. A river runs below the red mountains. Waite associates this card with "stability, power, aid, protection, a great person, conviction, reason." Case has "stability, power, reason, ambition, oversight, control." The Emperor addresses Ouspensky: "I am the Great Law. I am the Name of God. The four letters of His Name are in me and I am in everything. I am in the four principles, I am in the four

---

[11] Bailey, 1960, loc.cit.
[12] Elani Temperance, http://baringtheaegis.blogspot.com/2017/10/the-doves-of-aphrodite.html. 2023.

elements. I am in the four seasons, I am in the four quarters of the earth. I am in the four signs of the Tarot. I am action, I am resistance, I am completion, I am result. For him who knows the way to see me, there are no mysteries on the earth." In the Pholarcos deck, The Emperor is shown as a Native American chief with an open eye at his chest and a crown of vegetation; behind him is a full blue orb. He holds a mirror in his left hand, while another mirror is behind him. Sorrenti states, "The Emperor's two mirrors detect the archetypal traffic both above and below, within and without. Every small structure and great palace has stable foundations with blue spirit arrows that transpire from within the paneling, instructions in stone, long-sought order. Everything runs smoothly and his scepter hums a good song for all. As he leads, he remembers to harmonize with cosmic law, lest deep animal groans haunt his sleep." Key 4 is the first of the zodiacal Keys, attributed to the Fire sign of Aries ruled by Mars, the key for which is C major. The keynote from *Esoteric Astrology* for Aries is "I come forth, and from the plane of mind, I rule."[13] This Key is associated with the Hebrew letter Heh, the Window, which in the Sefer Yetzirah is attributed to the Constituting Intelligence, and to the quality of sight or vision. In the body, it represents the head. The Emperor corresponds to the figure in Freemasonry known as the Grand Architect of the Universe.[14] He has delimited a field of personal experience and is contemplating the highest manifestation of it while holding firm the lower. He has confined the waters of the High Priestess into a river course – as in Psalm 29: "The Lord sitteth upon the Flood."[15] By this act of limitation he makes them useful rather than overwhelming. He sets everything in its proper place at the dawn of Creation.

The piece, in C major throughout, begins with an appropriately martial Allegretto fanfare introduction in 2/4 time, which transitions into 4/4 with a further fanfare, leading to the main theme, derived inspirationally from Josquin des Pres' "Vive le Roi"[16]. It is scored for a brass ensemble consisting of 2 horns, 2 trumpets, trombone, and tuba, accompanied by snare drum and bass drum. In addition to the Josquin des Pres tune, it is made up of only 2 dream segments (the fanfares) and is 2:35 minutes long.

---

[13] Alice Bailey, 1951, op. cit., p. 108.
[14] Freemasonry Network, https://freemasonry.network/freemasonry-and-god/great-architect-universe/.
[15] Psalms 29:10.
[16] Josquin des Pres, loc.cit.

Key 5 – The Hierophant

In the Case deck, The Hierophant, dressed as a pope, sits on an indoor throne, attended by two tonsured priests whom he blesses. Their robes bear images of lilies and roses. Waite associates this card with "marriage alliance, captivity, servitude, mercy and goodness, inspiration." Case has "intuition, teaching, inspiration, marriage, alliance, occult force voluntarily invoked." Ouspensky says, "He speaks only for those who have ears to hear. But woe unto them who believe that they hear before they have really heard, or hear that which he does not say, or put their own words in place of his words. They will never receive the keys of understanding." In the Pholarcos deck, The Hierophant is a woman bare to the waist, facing a burning phoenix. The lower part of her body is a horse. Two balls containing spirals – in the Pholarcos deck these are symbols of the Earth element – are behind her, and a white regenerated phoenix flies upward from the lower of the two. Sorrenti states, "Before the temple, mosque, synagogue, church, the caves were homes to sacred ritual, a lair of wonder. . . Preside over the Mysteries so they may make a map for you." Key 5 is attributed to the Earth sign of Taurus ruled by Venus, the key for which is C#/Db major. The keynote for Taurus from *Esoteric Astrology* is "I see, and when the eye is opened, all is light."[17] This Key is associated with the Hebrew letter Vav, the Nail, which in the Sefer Yetzirah is attributed to the Triumphant and Eternal Intelligence, and to the quality of hearing. In the body, it represents the ear and the throat. The Hierophant is the One Initiator, before whom candidates for spiritual advancement stand. He has emerged from the grey stone behind him, and having emerged, he is a higher vessel for the power that flows in him and through him. He is the revealer of the Mysteries, the conveyor of the hidden knowledge from above. He is the Stone (Petrus/Peter, the first Pope), which in Hebrew is Eben, which combines the words for Father (Ab) and Son (Ben). He performs the Sacred Marriage of the Two into One. The nail is the symbol of this union, as the letter Vav in Hebrew is the copular, "and". The Hierophant's face in the Case deck bears a striking resemblance to Master 7 8.

This is a very slow, Lento piece in Db major scored for vibraphone, chimes, piano, and bass drum. It begins with a syncopated opening in 5/4 time, followed by a highly chromatic section which is interrupted by a loud sounding of the chimes. There is a concluding lyrical section in 3/4 time. The piece is made up of 3 dream segments and is 3:30 minutes long.

---

[17] Alice Bailey, 1951, op. cit., p.403.

Key 6 – The Lovers

In the Case deck, the naked Lovers stand beneath two trees, the woman's on the left with five pieces of fruit and a serpent coiled around it; the man's on the right with twelve flame-shaped leaves. The archangel Raphael blesses them both from above. Waite associates this card with "attraction, love, beauty, trials overcome." Case has "attraction, beauty, love, harmony of inner and outer life." In the Pholarcos deck, the naked lovers embrace; the man has the symbol of entwined serpents tattooed on his left forearm. Sorrenti states that they "heat their souls to every color. You plunge and surge onto a shore of deep belonging. Now you are vast, the waters of love dissolve your mold yet passion is always glistening inside you, setting a course for life, not only now. Within the fiery dragon of the heart is the lookout point." Key 6 is attributed to the Air sign of Gemini ruled by Mercury, which is associated with D major and its relative B minor. The keynote for Gemini from *Esoteric Astrology* is "I recognize my other self, and in the waning of that self, I grow and glow."[18] This Key is associated with the Hebrew letter Zayin, the Sword, which in the Sefer Yetzirah is attributed to the Disposing Intelligence, and to the quality of smell. In the body, it represents the lungs. The voices of the Many are reduced to the voices of the Two, and then the voice of the One is heard, harmonizing them. It is necessary to order the chaos of thoughts present in the Empress' womb. This is done by setting up a pair of opposites. The thoughts will then be attracted to one or the other and constellate around them, giving them energy. This is the secret of the ellipse or egg, which it is not a sphere, but has two centroids. Only when the opposites are delineated, and discriminated, can the Uniter, the Healer (Raphael, the Healer of God) appear and bring them into harmony with one another. The tree behind the woman is the familiar Tree of Duality (the knowledge of good and evil). But the tree behind the man is the Tree of Life, with its twelve flames, and this tree is made by the hand of Man, with the help of the Hand of God. Yet the influence of the angel descends upon them both equally. This is the way of aspiration, of the beginning of the Path which leads from the Garden of Eden to the as yet untrodden mountain.

The piece is scored for woodwind quintet. It begins with a descending, plaintive theme in B minor, Lento, in 4/4 time for oboe, accompanied by bassoon, followed by a highly chromatic section, in which each instrument's upward scale ends in a statement of the "love-potion" leitmotiv from Wagner's *Tristan und Isolde*[19]. As is well known from the Prelude to that music-drama, the key of the opening is indeterminate, and only later resolves – this indeterminacy is carried into the Tarot music, with a further set of chromatic ascending and descending scales – as in the middle section of Key 5 – at an Andante tempo, which end in a restatement of the "love-potion" theme for all instruments. This is followed by a series of arpeggios played over the opening theme of the Liebestod from *Tristan und Isolde* and over the descending opening theme. Following this, there is a transition to 6/8 time for a section, followed by a final section in 4/4 which features an

---

[18] Alice Bailey, 1951, op. cit., p.370.
[19] Richard Wagner, op. cit. Libretto. Angel Records, New York, album 3588 E/L. p. 6.

obbligato flute playing the final Liebestod theme over arpeggios, ending in the ascending "Tristan" leitmotiv for all instruments – an inversion of the opening theme of the piece. The piece is made up of 12 dream segments, in addition to the Wagner quotes, and is 2:50 minutes long.

Key 7 – The Chariot

In the Case deck, The Chariot, driven by a pair of sphinxes, one white, one black, carries the armored charioteer away from a city. Waite associates this card with "succor, providence, also war, triumph, presumption, vengeance, trouble." Case has "triumph, victory, and the like." Ouspensky says,"He drives the chariot by the strength of his will and of the magic sword, but the tension of his will may weaken and the sphinxes may pull in different directions and tear him and his chariot in two." In the Pholarcos deck, the body of the Chariot is an open lotus, and the Charioteer is an Egyptian Pharaoh. Sorrenti states, "It may not be strictly legal but this primed driver can swerve you through any terrain, no frontiers impregnable, no incline too steep, no fog too thick." Key 7 is attributed to the sign of Cancer ruled by the Moon, a Water sign associated with Eb major. The keynote for Cancer from *Esoteric Astrology* is "I build a lighted house and therein dwell."[20] This Key is associated with the Hebrew letter Cheth, the Fence, which in the Sefer Yetzirah is attributed to the Intelligence of the House of Influence, and to the quality of speech. In the body, it represents the chest and the stomach. The Chariot exemplifies three different types of motion: the wheels move in a circle, the axle in a spiral, and the chariot itself in a straight line. These correspond to the Three Rays of Aspect: Active Intelligence (circle), Consciousness (spiral), and Will (straight line): "When the rotary, the forward, and the spiral cyclic movements are working in perfect synthesis then the desired vibration will have been reached."[21] The keyword is <u>articulation</u>, without which speech is impossible, from *artis* + *culo*, to cook the art, or to expose it to the tempering fires of Spirit. A hymn: "When Thou ridest forth in the morning in Thy chariot of Glory, the Heavens proclaim the Majesty of Thy Victorious Strength; the Earth trembles under Thy feet at the sound of Thy approach; and all creation sings Thy great praise. For Thou art the Conqueror, the Vanquisher of Night, and All is before Thee. Hail!"

The piece is scored for piano, cello, and oboe. This is unusual for the Tarot music, as only the cello, as a stringed instrument, belongs to the Water element. As is well known, Beethoven composed a series of twelve variations in G major for cello and piano on Handel's aria "See, the Conquering Hero Comes" from the latter's oratorio *Judas Maccabeus*[22]. While not presuming to copy the master, this piece is comprised of a set of seven variations on the same theme, all in Eb major

---

[20] Alice Bailey, 1951, op. cit., p.343.
[21] Alice Bailey, *A Treatise on Cosmic Fire*. Lucis Publications, New York, 1925. pp. 1031-1035.
[22] John Magnum, https://www.laphil.com/musicdb/pieces/4455/variations-for-cello-and-piano-on-see- the-conquering-hero-comes-from-handels-judas-maccabaeus. n.d.

or its relative minor, C minor. It opens with a brief Maestoso fanfare in 4/4 time, followed by a statement of the theme. The first variation, Cantabile, tosses the theme back and forth among the three instruments. The second, Molto Allegro, features the theme in the piano while the other instruments play rapid triplets over it. The third variation, Allegro, is in 3/4 time. Variation four, Moderato, returns to 4/4 time, and alternates the theme between the oboe and cello while the piano plays scales. Variation five, Vivace, breaks the theme up into brief statements tossed back and forth among the three instruments. Variation six, Andante, provides yet further excursions on the theme. Variation seven, Allegro, returns to 3/4 time, and as in variation five the theme is segmented into brief phrases, but in C major, associated with C minor. The piece concludes with a restatement of the Maestoso fanfare and the original theme in Eb major, again in 4/4. The piece is comprised of 8 dreams, and is by far the longest of the Major Arcana pieces, at 10:25 minutes.

Key 8 – Strength

In the Case deck, a white-robed woman opens the mouth of a red lion, on a plain. An infinity sign hovers over her head. Waite associates this card with "power, energy, action, courage, magnanimity." Case has "action, courage, power, control of the life-force." Ouspensky says, "Here you pass into the realm of mysteries. For a consciousness that is aware of the sign of Eternity above it, there are no obstacles, nor can there be any resistance from the infinite." In the Pholarcos deck, the woman and the lion gaze in the same direction, "as her features become increasingly leonine", while there is a scene below of a lion king, a woman with a clawed hand, and a woman dropping a pair of suns. A decapitated female head is in the upper left. Sorrenti[23] states, "Inside your belly the lion's hunger [is] insatiable, its eyes yellow alarm, claws ready-made scythes. It will not hesitate to rip right through you and make a mockery of your life in order to find food. It will have you unless you turn and look into those eyes, offer of yourself. Exchange on its own terms. Then it will, like the cards of old, open its mouth for you and let you take what you need when you need it . . . Do not think you can bypass the wild center – it generates your will to live." Key 8 is attributed to the Fire sign of Leo, which is associated with the key of E major. The keynote for Leo from *Esoteric Astrology* is "I am That and That am I."[24] This Key is associated with the Hebrew letter Teth, the Serpent, which in the Sefer Yetzirah is attributed to the Intelligence of the Secret of Works, and to the quality of taste. In the body, it represents the heart. In alchemy, the Red Lion represents the stage of the Work which involves passion, and the woman is opening the mouth of the lion to express this passion in a controlled way. This involves the utilization of the mind – manas – for only the mind has the power to tame the animal nature. Now that the lower fires have been quenched by opening up the higher fires, the lower fires are put to work by the

---

[23] Following some traditional decks, Sorrenti interchanges Keys 8 and 11, so this is her Key 11.
[24] Alice Bailey, 1951, op. cit., p.311.

purified disciple; they need to be feared no longer. All of the energy for this flows from the Sun, the ruler of Leo. This tremendous energy flows in waves and is the source of all activity.

The piece in E major is scored for two trumpets and two euphoniums (horns could be substituted for the latter). It is a rondo in 4/4 time, Andante, with the rondo theme a characteristic ascending and descending triad, played staccato. The excursions are somewhat more lyrical, but brief. The piece is comprised of 5 dreams, with a duration of 2:25 minutes.

Key 9 – The Hermit

In the Case deck, The Hermit, robed in grey, with his blue crown in the shape of the letter Yod, stands atop a mountain to guide pilgrims through the dark night with the light from his lantern. Waite associates this card with "prudence, also and especially treason, dissimulation, corruption, roguery." Case has "wisdom from above, prudence, circumspection." In the Pholarcos deck, the Hermit is a bearded, dark-skinned elder, with the image of a horned goddess, whom Sorrenti names "Shapeshifter", above him[25]. Sorrenti states, "His brain is aligned with the heart as the dragon-snake crosses through his eye and rises like the kundalini serpent. He governs what seems permanent: bones, architecture and the contours of your incarnation, everything you build upon—from here, if you negotiate, you may travel your soul to the matrix of stars, the patterns spiraling in and out of form." Key 9 is attributed to the Earth sign of Virgo ruled by Mercury, which is associated with the key of F major. The keynote for Virgo from *Esoteric Astrology* is "I am the Mother and the Child. I, God, I, matter am."[26] This Key is associated with the Hebrew letter Yod, the Hand, which in the Sefer Yetzirah is attributed to the Intelligence of Will, and to the quality of touch. In the body, it represents the intestines, where food is digested: the "house of bread" (Bethlehem). In Sefer Yetzirah, all of the letters of the Hebrew alphabet are said to be "crowned", and the crown is the letter Yod itself, which is the Hermit's crown. Its tip extends into the Infinite and its base is the Earth. While the background of this card is a dark night, this is one of the brightest cards in the deck![27] The Hermit stands at the top of the mountain, the dwelling place of Spirit, and from this etheric height lets shine forth the beaconing light. An affirmation: "I am the blue-lidded daughter of sunset. I am the naked brilliance of the voluptuous night sky. To me! To me!" As the Hand of God is all that we can perceive from below, for it is the closest to us, we sometimes forget that the Body of God is much larger and takes in the whole of manifestation, though this is hidden in mystery.

---

[25] This figure is also used for the backs of all the cards in the Pholarcos deck.
[26] Alice Bailey, 1951, op. cit., p.252.
[27] In both the Waite and Case decks, the Hermit is shown against a dark background, but in the Pholarcos Tarot he is surrounded by white light – Sorrenti's dream image accords with my 50-year old Tarot notebook impressions!

The piece in F major is a rondo scored for two glockenspiels, vibraphone, and marimba, and is in 9/8 time. The tempo is slow, Misterioso. The marimba sets up a pulsating ostinato undertone over which the vibraphone plays a melody. This is then repeated by the two glockenspiels. The same pulsating rhythm is carried through the three excursions, and on beyond the last iteration of the theme, fading off into silence. The piece is comprised of 3 dreams, and is 5:40 minutes in length. This was one of the earliest pieces completed for the Musical Dream Tarot.

Key 10 – The Wheel of Fortune

In the Case deck, the orange Wheel, the color of the Sun, is adorned with letters in Latin script making up the word "Tarot" (or "Tora") and in Hebrew script the Tetragrammaton, and with astrological and alchemical symbols. A blue sphinx with a sword stands at its summit, a yellow serpent descends on the left, and the red figure of the Egyptian god Hermanubis ascends on the right, while the symbols of the "Four Living Creatures" of the Chariot of God in Ezekiel (Bull, Lion, Eagle, and Man)[28], which represent all four elements (Earth, Fire, Water, and Air, respectively) and the four Fixed Signs of the Zodiac (Taurus, Leo, Scorpio, and Aquarius) grace the corners. Waite associates this card with "destiny, fortune, success, luck, felicity." Case has "destiny, good fortune, turn for the better." Ouspensky says, "Everything goes, everything returns, eternally rolls the wheel of being. Everything dies, everything blossoms forth again; eternally runs the year of being. Everything breaks, everything is united anew; eternally builds itself the same house of being. Everything parts, everything meets again; the ring of being remains eternally true to itself." In the Pholarcos deck, a female figure in a birthing position generates the symbols of the wheel of the zodiac. Sorrenti states, "Here spins every fate and our dance of freedom within its cycle. Throw the dice, the runes, the I Ching coins; they will all speak of this rising and this falling within which the creative spirit flows." Key 10 is attributed to the planet Jupiter, which is the ruler of Sagittarius (Ab major). Jupiter expresses the Second Ray of Love/Wisdom, for which the Word of Power is "I see the greatest light."[29] This Key is associated with the Hebrew letter Kaph, the Fist, which in the Sefer Yetzirah is attributed to the Rewarding Intelligence of Those Who Seek, and to the qualities of wealth and poverty. On the Qabbalistic Tree of Life, Jupiter is associated with Mercy (Chesed). In the system of the chakras I learned In SOTGO, Jupiter is related to the solar plexus center. The Wheel represents the game of manifestation, ruled by the Sphinx as the mother of Form. The serpent represents the descent of spirit into matter, and Hermanubis represents the ascent back into spirit. The clouds round about the Wheel are the result of the evaporation of moisture by the heat of the Sun, which precipitate in the form of rain. They are Patanjali's "raincloud of knowable things,"[30] the source of all seed thoughts. It is from them that we draw knowledge of the cycles

---

[28] Ezekiel 1:4-28.
[29] Alice Bailey, 1960, op.cit., p. 516.
[30] Alice Bailey, 1927, loc. cit.

of Nature which are represented in the Wheel. The Wheel is also the cycle of life and death, the eternal interplay, which in Divine Beneficence shapes the world. To embrace the turning of the Wheel is to accept Life whole, both the right and the left, as manifestations of the Divine Plan.

Ab major was used for almost all of the music, with only a brief excursion into B major[31], and another into C major, the major key of the relative minor of Eb major, C minor. Sagittarius is a Fire sign, but because the Case and Waite decks' Key 10 displays the symbols of all four elements, instruments from all four orchestral groups were used in the composition: guitar, trumpet, horn, English horn, viola, and cello. Numerous ascending and descending scales depict the inexorable turning of the Wheel. Some of the descents are quite precipitous, underlain in most sections by a driving rhythm in the lower instruments. This is a more complex piece than most in the set, with both time signature and key signature changes. It begins in 4/4 time, Allegro, but the same ascending-descending scale structure is then played in 6/8 time. It then returns to 4/4 rhythm, and begins a rondo for which the theme is a set of scalar calls and responses between instrument pairs. An excursion in 3/4 time follows, followed by the rondo theme in 4/4 again. Another excursion in B major is followed by a final statement of the rondo theme, after which the piece returns to the opening theme in Ab. The piece is comprised of 9 dreams, and is 5:40 minutes long.

Key 11 – Justice

In the Case deck, the unblindfolded figure of Justice sits on a throne in an interior space, holding her balance in one hand and a sword in the other. Waite associates this card with "equity, rightness, probity, executive." Case has "strength and force, but arrested, as in the act of judgment. Legal affairs, lawsuits." Ouspensky says, "You are seeing Truth. Everything is weighed in these scales. That sword is eternally lifted in defence of justice and nothing can escape it." In the Pholarcos deck[32], the crowned figure of Justice, with eyes closed and wearing a feathered shawl, holds a mechanical bird, which is cawing. A second female figure, dressed as a ballerina, looks upon the scene from the right. Sorrenti states, "Careful honing of winged thought, there are patterns to weave along the nerve cells, soul grammar to consider." Key 11 is attributed to the Air sign of Libra ruled by Venus, which is associated with the key of F# major. The keynote for Libra from *Esoteric Astrology* is "I choose the way that leads between the two great lines of force."[33] This Key is associated with the Hebrew letter Lamed, the Ox-Goad, which in the Sefer Yetzirah is attributed to the Faithful Intelligence, and to the quality of work or action. In the body, it represents the kidneys, which eliminate toxins. As the central point of the Major Arcana, and standing for the Air element, which balances fire and water, this Key represents the greatest test through which a man must pass. Each time

---

[31] In the older astrology, Jupiter was held also to rule Pisces (B major).
[32] As noted above, Sorrenti has this as Key 8.
[33] Alice Bailey, 1951, op. cit., p. 251.

he will come to a certain point on the Wheel of Life where he finds that he is in the presence of unswerving Justice, and must make a choice whether to follow the Divine Will or his own personal will. If he chooses the former, giving himself fully to self-surrender and the abnegation of his own personal will, he will achieve union with the Beloved. But if he chooses the latter, he is returned to the Wheel to circle around again. The goad (represented by the Sword) is grasped by the Spirit through the agency of Cosmic Consciousness. It herds those who had milled about with a lack of control and discrimination, and brings them back under the control of the shepherd once again.

The piece in F# major is a duet for clarinet and bassoon, Moderato. It opens in 3/4 time with a series of upward-sweeping runs for each instrument. This is followed by sections in 11/8 time alternating with sections in 4/4 time. This is the most atonal and modern-sounding of all of the Major Arcana pieces. The piece is comprised of 6 dreams, and is 3:40 minutes long.

Key 12 – The Hanged Man

In the Case deck, The Hanged Man is suspended by his foot from the upper bar of a wooden frame which resembles the Hebrew letter Tav. A bright aura surrounds his head, as his inverted position has resulted in enlightenment. Waite associates this card with "wisdom, trials, circumspection, discernment, sacrifice, intuition, divination, prophecy." Case has "in spiritual matters: wisdom, surrender to the inevitable. In material affairs: losses, reverses." Ouspensky says, "Behold, this is the man who has seen the Truth . . . It is for this that he went a long journey from trial to trial, from initiation to initiation, through failures and through falls. And now he has found Truth and has known himself." In the Pholarcos deck, the Hanged One is an androgynous figure, upside down, surrounded by vegetation and grapes, as butterflies stream from her/his head. Sorrenti compares this state to that of a chrysalis or cocoon hanging upside down, and she states, "An archaic lineage comes calling. It is your turn to allow control to flood away not knowing who you will be when it returns. The great river rushes through you. You are not alone in this surrender and everything moves in surprising ways . . ." Key 12 is the second of the elemental Major Arcana, and is attributed to Water. This Key is associated with the Hebrew letter Mem, Water, which in the Sefer Yetzirah is attributed to the Stable Intelligence. In modern decks Key 12 is associated with the planet Neptune, appropriately, as the god Neptune rules the Sea. Neptune, as noted above, expresses the Sixth Ray of Devotion and Idealism, the Word of Power for which is "The highest light controls."[34] The Hanged Man floats in the waters of Mem like a baby in a womb. The rope by which he is hanging is like an umbilical cord, the means by which nourishment can reach him. Although still within the womb of Mother Nature, he is able to perceive the light through the door of Her womb. The trees which form the support for the horizontal beam on which he hangs grew naturally, but their branches have been lopped off. As they are part of the letter

---

[34] Alice Bailey, 1960, op. cit., p. 518.

Tav, which is associated with Earth, these represent attachments to the Earth which have been eliminated. This process of elimination leads to the highest stage of yogic practice, Samadhi[35], which is sometimes translated as "suspension". The halo of light around the Hanged Man's head is evidence that he is in a state of Samadhi. This realization proceeds from the rejection of the personal will, then submission to the Divine Will, and finally to a first-hand knowledge that that Will is identical with his own, that there is no other Will power in all the Universe. "Between the sword (Key 11) and the scythe (Key 13), I stand steady; naught shall I fear, I, the Child born of a lotus, and my name is Silence."

The piece is scored for string quartet, Allegro. Of the three keys associated with the Water element (Eb, G, and B), only Eb and G were used. It opens in G major with a somewhat sentimental, flowing theme in 4/4 time. The pace picks up somewhat after that, and there is a transition into Eb major for another lively set of themes. The music transitions back to G major, for a waltz section in 3/4 time, which will be the dominant time signature for the rest of the piece. This then transitions into a section in Eb major, still in a flowing waltz tempo, expressing the watery nature of the Key. There is an abrupt interruption of this, again in 4/4 and in G major, by some rather jagged rhythms that are played both direct and in inversion – the Hanged Man, after all, is suspended upside down! The waltz is resumed, still in G major, and the original sentimental theme reemerges, in 3/4 time, at the end. The piece is comprised of 14 dreams, and is 6:30 minutes long.

Key 13 – Death

In the Case deck, the traditional skeleton mows down the severed heads and hands of his victims with his scythe, while a river flows off into the sunset – or, more probably, the sunrise. Waite associates this card with "end, mortality, destruction, corruption." Case has "contrarieties, sudden change, death." Ouspensky asks, "Does the sun know anything of the earth, of people of the sunset and sunrise? It goes its own way, over its own orbit, round an Unknown Centre. Life, Death, sunrise, sunset; are you not aware that all these are but the thoughts, dreams, and fears of the Fool?" In the Pholarcos deck, the black-robed figure of Death holds a glowing orb, from which an arc stretches in both directions, while a female supplicant approaches him in the dark forest of Psyche. Many white birds fly among the trees. Sorrenti states, "What you know turns inside out – you may not recognize this new place but it has great value . . . Keep your wits about you as you harvest metamorphosis." The Key is attributed to the Water sign of Scorpio ruled by Mars and/or Pluto, and is associated with the key of G major and its relative minor, E minor. The keynote for Scorpio from *Esoteric Astrology* is "Warrior I am, and from the battle I emerge triumphant."[36] This Key is associated with the Hebrew letter Nun, the Fish, which in the Sefer

---

[35] Alice Bailey, 1927, op. cit., IV.18.
[36] Alice Bailey, 1951, op. cit., p. 206.

Yetzirah is attributed to the Imaginative Intelligence, and with the quality of motion. In the body, it represents the genital organs. Death wanders in the dark fields of the manifested physical world, searching for the living Fish to cast it into the waters. When undeveloped, that fish is Behemoth, the Beast, but as it begins its motion up the spinal column (as displayed by the skeleton) it transforms into Leviathan,[37] the crooked serpent of consciousness, the bending river, until it reaches the head, as seen in the sunrise at the end of the river. The reference to the spinal column brings in the symbolism of the chakras, and in particular the sacral center, which is related to sexuality. It may be asked why sexuality is so closely linked to death, or why the icon for the god Shiva, the Lord of Destruction, is the phallus. But Death, in those religions like Hinduism which conceive of reincarnation, is only the prelude to the next life, whose manifestation is, of course, brought about by the union of the sexual organs. Thus, Death leads to new life, and it may be suggested that what the figure of Death is harvesting with his scythe is the morning dew, the precipitation of the water element. This dew nourishes the new life. The grin on the face of the skeleton suggests that he is a representative of the Great Laugh which was discussed under Key 0. This is the state of the Soul between incarnations. The rising Sun in the background is a symbol of the infinite Mercy of God, for when we eliminate the dross from our bodies and our minds it flows down the cosmic stream and is absorbed into the Sun, which consumes it utterly and returns it to us as rays of light, which we can make use of to eliminate yet more dross. Our role is only to direct this flow of energy, therefore is the body of the adept continually renewed. The Mercy of God (Chesed) is the limitless consumer of all that is gross and the producer of all that is subtle, for everything is of It and from It.

Most of the music for the Musical Dream Tarot is intended to express the moods associated with each Key, but the music for Key 13 is somewhat more programmatic. It describes the process of abstraction from physical incarnation which we call Death, somewhat reminiscent of the storyline in Richard Strauss' tone poem Tod und Verklaerung[38]. It is scored for string quartet, plus timpani and cymbals. The piece begins in E minor and is in 6/8 time throughout. It opens with a rather dynamic theme, Moderato, depicting the initial anguish of the process of abstraction, with some deliberate dissonances. There follows a section which is even more dissonant, reminiscent of some of the twelve-tone pieces of Schoenberg, which represents the actual breaking of the "silver cord" which binds the spiritual essence to the corporeal. The anguished theme returns, followed by a section in which the melody, though no longer dissonant, is punctuated by beats on the timpani and viola which replicate heart rhythms. These eventually fade away to be replaced by a sweeter melody in G major as the final disintegration proceeds and the Soul sails off into the sunrise. The piece is comprised of 7 dreams, and is 2:50 minutes long.

---

[37] Catherine Shainberg, *The Kabbalah of Light.* Inner Traditions, Rochester VT., 2022, passim.
[38] Richard Strauss, Tod und Verklaerung. https://www.youtube.com/watch?v=sBVbm7lxAhE.

Key 14 – Temperance

In the Case deck, the white-robed archangel Michael stands with one foot in the water and one on dry land, balancing the elements by pouring water from a jug onto the tawny lion to his right (Leo, fire) and applying a blazing torch to the eagle on his left (Scorpio, water). A rainbow arcs over his head. Behind the animals, a path leads to a crowned pass in the mountains. Waite associates this card with "economy, moderation, frugality, management, accommodation." Case has "combination, adaptation, economy, management." Ouspensky says, "Men think that everything is incessantly flowing in one direction. They do not see that everything eternally meets, that one thing comes from the past and another from the future, and that time is a multitude of circles turning in different directions. Understand this mystery and learn to distinguish the opposite currents in the rainbow stream of the present." In the Pholarcos deck, the angel has been replaced by a dark-haired female alchemist with a crown of very curly blonde hair. She appears to be mixing elements alchemically; she "discovers how new color harmonies make a whole." Sorrenti adds, "Cosmic order through communication. Stand at the liminal crossing, hold the threshold open for consciousness to change perspective." Key 14 is attributed to the Fire sign of Sagittarius ruled by Jupiter, which is associated with the key of Ab major, and its relative minor, F minor. The keynote for Sagittarius from *Esoteric Astrology* is "I see the goal. I reach that goal and then I see another."[39] This Key is associated with the Hebrew letter Samekh, the Tent-Peg, which in the Sefer Yetzirah is attributed to the Intelligence of Probation or Trial, and to the quality of wrath. In the body, it represents the thighs. The angel is the Middle Way between the pairs of opposites, and this narrow way is indicated by the arrow of Sagittarius, which is shot towards its mark. The jug of water is of clay, which is tempered by fire to create it. The lion's gaze is toward the pool of water, wherein he sees a reflection of the angel. This is accomplished by the flow of magnetic water down upon him. The eagle, however, looks directly at the angel himself, and this is done by means of the electric fire held above him. Water flows downward to its source (matter), while fire flows upwards to its source (spirit). The sign of Sagittarius leads to the winter solstice, the darkest part of the yearly cycle. "Thus, now as ever, I enter the Path of Darkness, if haply so I may attain the Light. Hail!"

The piece is scored for trumpet, horn, trombone, tuba, snare drum, and marimba, with an obbligato Bb clarinet. It is characterized by a driving dotted rhythm throughout almost the entire piece, suggestive of the onward drive of the Sagittarian. Most of the piece is in F minor, Moderato, but there is a section, with the obbligato clarinet, in F major, repeated by the brass instruments and even by the marimba, followed by the return of the F minor theme. An excursion in the same key follows, and the piece concludes with a restatement of the original theme on all instruments. The piece is comprised of 7 dreams, and is 3:25 minutes long.

---

[39] Alice Bailey, 1951, op. cit., p. 192.

Key 15 – The Devil

In the Case deck, the gross, earthy figure of the Devil (actually the archangel Auriel) holds a bestial man and woman chained to the half-cube on which he sits. But the chains around their necks are so loose that they could, if they wished, easily remove them. Waite associates this card with "ravage, violence, force, vehemence, extraordinary efforts, fatality, that which is predestined but not for this reason evil." Case has "bondage, materiality, necessity, force, fate." To Ouspensky, the Devil says, "I am Evil, in so far as evil can exist in this best of all worlds. In order to perceive me one must see crookedly, wrongly, and narrowly. Three paths lead to me: conceit, suspicion and accusation. My chief virtues are calumny and slander. I complete the triangle, the two other sides of which are death and time. In order to escape from this triangle it is only necessary to see that it does not exist." In the Pholarcos deck, The Devil's face is merely a grinning, horned mask, above which is a peacock with its tail displayed. Below is the image of a weeping woman whose head the mask is eating alive; her blood pours down her face. This image made its way into my dreaming after the completion of the project, and was the seed for a new composition, an oboe concerto. Sorrenti states, "can you bear to dance with your shadow, hold it close till it transforms into the riches of your being? This is the core of alchemy." Key 15 is attributed to the Earth sign of Capricorn ruled by Saturn, which is associated with the key of A major. The keynote for Capricorn from *Esoteric Astrology* is "Lost am I in light supernal, yet on that light I turn my back."[40] This Key is associated with the Hebrew letter 'Ayin, the Eye or the Well, which in the Sefer Yetzirah is attributed to the Renewing Intelligence, and to the quality of mirth. In the body, it represents the knees. The Devil represents a frozen moment in time, when the pulse is negative, but is generalized for all Eternity – the basic misconception that gives rise to Evil. He represents the Demiurge, the will-to-be no matter how. However, this will-to-be does not include balance in its drive into manifestation, and the personality – the human figures – is left in a primitive state. Because the female figure looks outward and not at the angel (as in Key 6), there is no balance to the relationship between her and the man. Rather than aiding them, the Devil raises his hand and gives a sign of discipline to hard, rigid, inflexible laws. This is the road of the old religions, whose adherents believe that their God is the only means of salvation. Thus they are chained to the half-truth of a single ideology. As Tennyson wrote, "The old order changeth, yielding place to new, and God fulfills Himself in many ways, lest one good custom should corrupt the world."[41] And the best way of exploding this crystallization of "good custom" is, in fact, mirth!

As noted in Chapter 7, almost all of the pieces composed for the Musical Dream Tarot are made up of multiple dream fragments. Key 15 is the exception; there was only a single dream, early in the process, which was combined with two inspirational elements: the Dies Irae theme from

---

[40] Alice Bailey, 1951, op. cit., p. 173.
[41] Alfred, Lord Tennyson, *Le Morte d'Arthur*. In *Idylls of the King*. Dover Publications, New York, 2004. I:417-419.

the Latin Mass and a theme from Stephen Schwartz's "Prepare Ye the Way of the Lord" from *Godspell*[42]. The piece is scored in A major for xylophone, vibraphone piano, tuba, and maracas.[43] The tone of the music is rather sly, after the fashion of a jazz swing tune. It begins with the maracas setting up the rhythm in 4/4 time, Allegro, shortly followed by the tuba stating the Dies Irae theme, which continues through most of the piece. The piano then chimes in with a swing theme which is repeated three times at increasing volume, to which is added the *Godspell* theme on the vibraphone, with embroidery by the xylophone. All of these drop out, one by one, leaving only the tuba on the *Godspell* theme, fading into silence. This piece is the shortest of the Major Arcana pieces, being only 1:35 minutes long.

Key 16 – The Tower

In the Case deck, the crowned Tower is struck by lightning emanating from the Sun, and two human figures, a man and a woman, fall from it, presumably to their deaths. Waite associates this card with "misery, distress, ruin, indigence, adversity, calamity, disgrace, deception." Case has "danger, conflict, unforeseen catastrophes, ambition." Ouspensky says, "Nature hates deceit, and man cannot subjugate himself to her laws. Nature is patient for a long time and then suddenly with one blow she annihilates all that goes against her." In the Pholarcos deck, a woman in blue has been split in two by a bolt of lightning; she seems suspended in the air. Sorrenti states, "Lightning strikes and splits your soul into a thousand colors. This is an awakening. Every particle gets charged and when you knit yourself back together, the transmissions work differently; you may need to learn a new language that bonds you with the world. Here is the complete annihilation, the revisioning, a new incarnation in your old body." Key 16 is attributed to the planet Mars, which is the ruler of the Fire sign Aries (C major) and the Water sign Scorpio (G major). Mars expresses the Sixth Ray of Devotion and Idealism, for which the Word of Power is "The highest light controls."[44] This Key is associated with the Hebrew letter Peh, the Mouth, which in the Sefer Yetzirah is attributed to the Active or Exciting Intelligence, and to the qualities of grace and sin. On the Qabbalistic Tree of Life, Mars is associated with Severity (Geburah). In the system of the chakras I learned In SOTGO, Mars is related to the sacral center. The Tower is the personality freed of its dross (the human figures), but its crown is a false crown which must be toppled by the lightning bolt of spirit so that it becomes a suitable temple for the Light. This is a reference to the Biblical Tower of Babel,

---

[42] Stephen Schwartz, loc. cit.

[43] I had at one point considered adding a baritone voice, as the dream which formed it was associated with the words, "Everything's sliding around" or "Everything's slipping away." However, that would have made this the only piece to include voice or text, so I eventually decided against this.

[44] Alice Bailey,1960, loc. cit.

which was a vain attempt to reach for the stars.[45] Its destruction resulted in the differentiation of languages (Peh, the mouth).

Both C major and G major are used in the piece, which is scored for trumpet, trombone, and euphonium. The opening, in C major in 4/4, Allegro, introduces a theme of triplets which will carry through much of the piece. The opening theme is then repeated in 6/8 time. There is a brief excursion into G major, followed by a return to C major and 4/4 time and a restatement of one of the opening themes. Another section in 6/8 follows, ending on a long, rapid descending figure in all three instruments, suggestive of the fall from the Tower. The piece is comprised of 7 dreams, and is 2:55 minutes long.

Key 17 – The Star

In the Case deck, the naked goddess Hathor, her legs in the right-angled position typical of Aquarius images for millennia[46], pours water from two vases, one onto the land and one into a pool, while eight stars shine in the sky above. Waite associates this card with "loss, theft, privation, abandonment . . . hope and bright prospects in the future." Case has "insight, hope, influence over others." Ouspensky says, "This is the imagination of Nature. Nature dreams, imagines, creates worlds. Learn to unite your imagination with her imagination, and nothing will ever be impossible for you." In the Pholarcos deck, the partially naked goddess is shown standing in meditation, with a star at her heart and eight stars on the upper hem of her robe. The symbols of waxing, full, and waning Moon are at the level of her womb, and water appears to be flowing from her breasts and from the ends of the robe. Sorrenti states, "The star at the center of her chest turns all tearful sorrow into crystal clear waters that irrigate the land. In accordance with lunar phases, life germinates and spirals up towards the star and its bright hope. The sage laughs into the deep cold pool until the water turns crystal clear again, gurgling regeneration." Key 17 is attributed to the Air sign of Aquarius ruled by Saturn and/or Uranus, which is associated with the key of Bb major. The keynote for Aquarius from *Esoteric Astrology* is "Water of life am I, poured forth for thirsty men."[47] This Key is associated with the Hebrew letter Tsaddi, the Fish-Hook, which in the Sefer Yetzirah is attributed to the Natural Intelligence, and to the quality of meditation. In the body, it represents the ankles, which form a right angle to the legs. The nature of the goddess's meditation is a cycle

---

[45] Genesis 11:1-9.

[46] As noted in Chapter Two, each of the Hebrew letters is also associated with a number, and the number for Tsaddi is 90, referencing the 90 degree angles in this pose. Ancient Mesopotamian images of figures in this pose, representing the god Dumuzi, are not uncommon; for example, this seal: https://www.google.com/search?q=akkadian+empire&tbm=isch&rlz=1C1GCEA_enUS836US836&hl=en&sa=X&ved=2ahUKEwijvrWdoMD8AhXlrnIEHRznAe8QrNwCKAB6BQgBEOIB&biw=1903&bih=937#imgrc=lYHxd1Lu5JXTjM.

[47] Alice Bailey, 1951, op. cit., p. 135.

of water or astral fluid, individuated into the four elements plus the ether. The water is lifted up into the vases and returns to the pool, an endless cycle, but as the vases are lifted the cycle spirals upwards. The vases represent the personality, through which the Life Force flows. The four streams which return to the pool refer to the waters which flow from the river Nahar which has its source in the Garden of Eden: the Pishon (spurter), Gichon (gusher), Tigris, and Euphrates.[48] As in this stage all the forces of the personality have been leveled to impersonal expressions, so also the Divine Idea is expressed geometrically in the eight-pointed star. The seven smaller stars represent the chakras. After the separative forces of the ego are overturned in Key 16, the shattered personality must be nourished with the Water of Life to restore it to activity.

This piece in Bb major is scored for a double wind quartet (two of each instrument) plus triangle (eight stars; 1+7 = 8). The opening theme, in 4/4 time, Andante, is stated canonically by pairs of instruments, followed by an inversion of the same theme. Figurations on these themes become more rapid, leading to a climax. This is followed by the simple restatement of the inverted theme, which leads to a more lively theme in 6/8 time. Following this, the original theme returns in 4/4 time, with similar figurations. The piece is comprised of 9 dreams, and is 5:30 minutes long.

Key 18 – The Moon

In the Case deck, under the light of the Full Moon, a dog and a wolf bay, while a crayfish emerges from a pool of water. A path leads from the pool beyond a pair of towers up to a pass between two mountains. Waite associates this card with "hidden enemies, danger, calumny, darkness, terror, deception, error." Case has "voluntary change, deception, hidden enemies." In the Pholarcos deck, a ballerina personifying the Moon hovers over a tidal pool of water, with a Chartres labyrinth figure behind her. Three owls that wax and wane are to the lower right, and the path to the mountains is to the upper left. Women in the four corners dance to the full moon. Sorrenti states, "Dionysian, electric . . . How many turnings of pattern and labyrinth can you float in at once?" Key 18 is attributed to the Water sign of Pisces ruled by Jupiter and/or Neptune, which is associated with the key of B major. The keynote for Pisces from *Esoteric Astrology* is "I leave the Father's home and turning back, I save."[49] This Key is associated with the Hebrew letter Qoph, the back of the head, which in the Sefer Yetzirah is attributed to the Corporeal Intelligence, and to the quality of sleep. In the body, it represents the feet. By concentrating just before going to bed on receiving in sleep the solution to one's problems, these will be solved and a way will be shown[50]. But if one can identify in one's self that force of which one's being is an expression, one can then relate to this force in all of Humanity; one becomes a part of Humanity. Then one

---

[48] Genesis 2:10-14.
[49] Alice Bailey, 1951, op. cit., p. 133.
[50] This is the method which gave rise to the *Musical Dream Tarot*!

can do the same practice for the problems of Humanity, thus "serve God day and night."[51] The mild face of the Moon is seen as a kindly overseer of the Path, like the Hermit (18 is 9 doubled), shedding his light for those who wander by night. The animals sense his presence: the dog and wolf by smell and the crayfish by its feelers. The presence of the Hermit is only implied by the path in the mountains; his feet have already trodden that path. The dog represents Art, as it has been domesticated, while the wolf represents Nature. The crayfish represents the aspirant, who, by slow and steady progress, makes his way between the extremes of Nature and Art. Beyond these figures is a gap between two towers, the gateway through which one must pass to attain the peak. This is a break in the security to which one is accustomed, a reversal at the portal of initiation before which the unprepared quail. Only one who is strong enough to break through the barrier of all human knowledge may attain to the final victory.

This piece is scored for string quartet. The overall mood is rather dreamy. An introductory gently rocking theme in 4/4 time, Lento, in B major, is followed by a section in 3/4 time, Moderato, with pulsating eighth notes played against a waltz tune. A set of chromatic scales is then set against pizzicato strings. The opening theme returns, again in Lento in 4/4 time. The piece is comprised of 5 dreams, and is 2:05 minutes long.

Key 19 – The Sun

In the Case deck, a pair of naked children dance in a faery ring under the light of the Sun, while five sunflowers are on the wall behind them. Waite associates this card with "material happiness, fortunate marriage, contentment." Case has "liberation, gain, riches." In the Pholarcos deck, a blonde male figure with gold radiating from his chest holds a blackbird, with a dotted circle, the symbol of the Sun, at its heart. Ouspensky says, "I saw that every ray of the Sun was the scepter of the Emperor which bore within it life. And I saw how beneath the sharp points of these rays the mystical flowers of the Waters were unfolding everywhere and how the rays penetrated into these flowers, and how the whole of Nature was continually born from the mysterious union of the two principles." Sorrenti states, "Plants, sea and sky lean into the sunlight around his head. Here's a quest encouraging you to find the hidden elixir, the unconcealed one. It surges you upwards into the elated world, now bright with substance. Give yourself to the inner marriage. Whatever you do in this life, find your essence and be true to it." Key 19, as its title suggests, is attributed to the Sun. The Sun expresses the Second Ray of Love/Wisdom, for which the Word of Power is "I see the greatest light."[52] This Key is associated with the Hebrew letter Resh, the head, which in the Sefer Yetzirah is attributed to the Collective Intelligence, and to the qualities of fruitfulness and sterility. On the Qabbalistic Tree of Life, the Sun is associated with Beauty (Tiphareth). In

---

[51] Revelations 7:15.
[52] Alice Bailey, 1960, op. cit., p. 516.

the system of the chakras I learned In SOTGO, the Sun is related to the crown center, above the center of the head. The children are the face of the Sun for the mineral, vegetable, and animal kingdoms, as well as for the average man, symbolized by the fact that four of the five sunflowers are turned towards them. Continually merged in the Sun's aura, their union is the source of all light, love, and power in our solar system. The sparks which are thrown off from their friction are the celestial rain which creates and destroys the planets – this is the source of Cosmic Fire. But their own source comes from beyond the system, for they, too, are a replica or spark of Divine Radiance. On the other side of the wall is an abyss, as behind the High Priestess there is a sea. Like the Fool, they dance near the edge of this abyss under the Sun. But the experience which they have gained – the bricks in the wall – stands between them and it. The fifth sunflower opens its flower directly over the abyss, pointing to that which lies beyond human experience. The Sun is a mandala, a wind rose with sixteen rays. It is not the twelve-rayed zodiac, because the zodiac must be transcended to be able to radiate in all directions. This also suggests that Humanity is not limited to any one religion or dogma, but that we should honor them all for the light which is within them and take what is needed for our spiritual and material nourishment.

The piece is scored for trumpet, horn, trombone, tuba, and hand cymbals. Since this is a Fiery orb, all three of the keys assigned to Fire signs (C major, E major, and F minor) are used in it. The opening section, in 4/4, Vivace, is in F minor and is somewhat somber and plodding in mood. This transitions into a livelier section in E major, followed by a key change to C major which transitions into a more dance-like section in 6/8 time. This transitions back into E major for the remainder of the piece. The Sun's warmth has dispelled all of the somber mood of the introduction! The piece is comprised of 13 dreams, and is 3:40 minutes in length.

Key 20 – Judgement

In the Case deck, on an Arctic sea, a man, woman, and child rise from their coffins, while the archangel Gabriel rouses them from death with the Seven-Ray blast of his trumpet. Waite associates this card with "change of position, renewal, outcome." Case has "decision, renewal, determines a matter." Ouspensky says, "In the sound of the trumpet I felt the smile of the Empress. And in the opening graves I saw the unfolding flowers, and in the extended hands I smelt the fragrance of flowers. And I understood the mystery of birth in death." In the Pholarcos deck, a Polynesian woman emerging from a tree stands within a garden filled with tame animals: a fox, a lion, a snake, an owl, an eagle, a cat, and two other birds. Sorrenti states, "here you are embraced by the community of beings. The dialogue deepens, expands, consciousness will never rest." Key 20 is the third of the elemental Keys, assigned to the Fire element, and the piece employs two of the Fire sign keys (C and E major). However, some astrologers also assign this Key to the planet Pluto, which along with Mars is one of the rulers of Scorpio (G major), and given the pictorial theme of resurrection in the Key, the association with Key 13 is obvious. Pluto expresses the First Ray of Will/Power, for which the Word of Power is "I assert the fact."[53] This Key is associated with the Hebrew letter Shin, the tooth, which in the Sefer Yetzirah is attributed to the Perpetual Intelligence. The whole motion of the Key is upwards; the seven rays emanating from the angel's trumpet not only descend but draw the figures – especially the child – into the mouth of the instrument. In esotericism, this upward motion is referred to as the Antahkarana, the inner thread, which is constructed out of mental substance from the integrated personality to the Soul and then to the higher planes. The method of construction differs according to which of the Seven Rays dominates.[54] The coffin of the child is a cube, like the cubes on which the High Priestess and the Emperor sit. Therefore his power is concealed inside the center at the base of the spine. It arises from the earthly grave through the employment of sound vibrations. These must first overthrow (Key 16) his parents, who held him down in the past. Only when these two are cast down and are submissive will the top of the cube fly open and the child emerge victorious. Then those parental functions serve as ministers to the Light. The trumpet of the Inner Voice overthrows the false structures of the personality and reveals the true Sonship.

The piece is scored for 2 trumpets, horn, trombone, euphonium, chimes, and timpani. The archangel Gabriel is associated with the Water element. For this reason, additional sections in G major and in C minor (the relative minor of Eb major) are used. It opens with a somewhat plaintive, gloomy, descending theme in C minor, in 3/4 time, Moderato, in the trombone, followed by the first trumpet, as if to express the sorrow at leaving this world. This is answered in G major by a similar theme on the horn and second trumpet, expressing the joy of integrating with a higher, more spiritual world. The tonality descends back into the minor, and the sequence repeats. The horn picks up the plaintive theme, followed ascending chromatic scales in the trombone, leading to a key change to a section in 4/4 in the brighter key of E major, which transitions in turn into C major and then G major, where it remains for the rest of the piece. The piece is comprised of 10 dreams, and is 5:45 minutes long.

---

[53] Ibid., p. 515.
[54] Ibid, pp. 501-518.

Key 21 – The World

In the Case deck, a mostly naked human figure, whose androgyny is concealed by a veil over her/his genital organs, dances within the confines of an oval wreath, holding glowing spirals in his/her hands. As in Key 10, the Case deck's Key 21 has the "Four Living Creatures" (Bull, Lion, Eagle, and Man) at its corners, representing the four elements. Waite associates this card with "assured success, route, voyage, emigration, flight, change of place." Case has "synthesis, success, change of place." In the Pholarcos deck, a pregnant woman, whose hair is a bird of paradise, is partly enclosed by a circle radiating from the light in her womb. The circle is an astrological chart. From a mountain below, a pair of entwined serpents rises to the level of her solar plexus, containing within their coils the symbols of the four elemental weapons (wand, cup, sword, pentacle). Sorrenti states, "Presence of fertility everywhere. Red is for coming to life, sacrum, mars, we live in a world of correspondence, we only think we are alone." Key 21, the final Key in the set of Major Arcana, is assigned to the planet Saturn, which is the ruler of the Earth sign Capricorn (A major). Saturn expresses the Third Ray of Active Intelligence, for which the Word of Power is "Purpose itself am I."[55] This Key is associated with the Hebrew letter Tav, the Cross, which in the Sefer Yetzirah is attributed to the Administrative Intelligence, and to the qualities of dominion and slavery. On the Qabbalistic Tree of Life, Saturn is associated with Understanding (Binah). In the system of the chakras I learned In SOTGO, Saturn is related to the center at the base of the spine. Here the Fool has taken the step over the edge of the Abyss and found that he/she is not bound by gravity, but is fully self-supporting. The 22 leaves of the wreath correspond to the 22 letters of the Hebrew alphabet and the 22 Major Arcana, but half of them descend (the Sutratma or involutionary thread) and half ascend (the Antahkarana) – also symbolized by the two spirals held by the dancer. All of the Keys have striven on earth to produce this final flower.

Because in the Waite and Case decks the "Four Living Creatures" are at the corners of the Key, representing the four elements, this piece is scored for one instrument from each group: horn (Fire), viola (Water), clarinet (Air), and harp (Earth), plus snare drum and bass drum (also Earth, as Saturn is related to that element). The entire piece is in A major, Molto Allegro, and begins in 4/4 time. Its mood celebrates the completion of the evolutionary process, with long runs of sixteenth notes. These continue into a more waltz-like section in 3/4 time. The final section is a reiteration of the long runs, but still in 3/4 time. The piece is comprised of 11 dreams, and is 2:15 minutes long.

---

[55] Ibid, p. 517.

✦ 9 ✦

The Minor Arcana – Wands

A total of 155 dreams were associated with Wands: 121 with dream texts, 27 without dream texts, and 7 duplicates. Although potentially the Fire element keys of E and Ab major could have been used for these compositions, all of them are either in C major or in its relative minor, A minor. Altogether, the fourteen Wands pieces are 49:30 minutes in length.

Ace of Wands

In the Waite deck, a hand issuing from a cloud grasps a stout Wand. Waite associates this card with creation, invention, enterprise . . . principle, beginning, source, birth, family, origin . . . money, fortune, inheritance." Case has "energy, strength, enterprise, principle, beginning." In the Pholarcos deck, there is a hoodwinked, androgynous figure, whose crown consists of galloping horses' heads. A gecko swerves around the Aries glyph on the figure's cheek. Sorrenti states, "that which ignites potency, engenders vision, pumps action . . . Here roars conquest, the spark of creation, what can you imagine and what can you become?" Common dream themes include rectilinear shapes (3), wife (3), a bedroom (2), campus (2), students (2), authority figures (2), house/home (2), rock/stone (2), and the colors green (2) and yellow/gold (2).

This piece, mostly in 3/4 time, Andante, is scored for horn and trombone. It begins with a stately waltz, which gradually becomes livelier. There is a return to the original pace, followed by a brief section in 4/4 time, a return to 3/4, and it concludes with the original tune. The piece is comprised of 9 dreams, and its duration is 6:05 minutes, the longest of the Minor Arcana pieces.

Two of Wands

In the Waite deck, a tall man looks from a battlemented roof over sea and shore. He holds a globe in his right hand, and a staff in his left rests on the battlement; another is fixed in a ring. Waite associates this card with "riches, fortune, magnificence . . . physical suffering, disease, chagrin, sadness, mortification." Case has "dominion." In the Pholarcos deck, two horses forming out of incandescent flame and light face one another, with a serpent above on whose body is the word "potency". The upper right corner contains a spiral with the symbols for Saturn, Sun, and Moon in a vertical row, and two Aries symbols. The spiral, which is repeated on all of the 2s, 6s, and 10s in this deck, is, as Sorrenti states, "a reminder of our incarnation and development in earthly existence. Saturn is at the threshold as Lord of Manifestation and Grand Architect of the physical plane. The spiraling takes us into Moon, the soul-making in lunar cyclical time and emotional tides. Her Moon is a sacred body-vessel in which we experience what gets transcribed to soul. The ongoing movement carries all this substance to the ever-present Sun, the enlivening essence and core light of the heart." Sorrenti states of this Key, "Yearn for me, I am your West, your undiscovered territory, your untamable song of plenty, uncharted far horizon, the percussive calling of your life." "Song of plenty" (or "plenty of songs") certainly characterizes the Musical Dream Tarot – and this was the second card which I drew at the 2021 dream conference in answer to my question, "what is my next project?"[1] Common dream themes include dwellings (2), cultural groups (2), young women (2), male figures (2), and the color red/copper (2).

This piece is a series of variations on a simple theme, mostly in 4/4 time, Allegro, and is scored for Bb trumpet and trombone. It begins in 4/4 with a statement of the theme, around which four variations are developed, shared back and forth between the two instruments. These morph into a brief excursion in 3/4 time, on a similar theme. With the return of the original theme in 4/4 time, there is a more lively set of variations, followed by a final statement of the original theme. The piece is comprised of 10 dreams and is 3:20 minutes in length.

Three of Wands

In the Waite deck, a calm, stately figure, with his back turned, is looking from a cliff's edge at ships passing over the sea. Three staves are planted in the ground, and he leans slightly on one of them. Waite associates this card with "established strength, enterprise, effort, trade, discovery, commerce." Case also has "established strength." In the Pholarcos deck, there is a series of three ballet dancers, one male, two female, beneath a flowing curtain of creative outpouring marked "passion" emanating from the middle ballerina, who is held up by three serpents. The words "divine song" are below. Sorrenti states, "Inspiration has taken hold and burns by the blue-white winds of spirit. The arrow is shot, movement splinters through the air, your heart is in the generous dance. Trust sweet blessings and the urge to amplify. Creation is on a confident spin of discovery." Common dream themes include rooms (3), houses of worship (2), and the colors red (2) and white (2). Decision or choice (2) was a common emotion.

This piece is in 4/4 time throughout, Vivace, and is scored for horn, two Bb trumpets, trombone, and euphonium. It begins with a syncopated rhythm in the euphonium, which is carried throughout the piece by various instruments. Above this, a noble tune emerges for the horn, which forms the basis of a consistent melody underlain by figurations and arpeggios in the other instruments. This melody also recurs in the Four of Wands music, and is the only example of a repeated theme in the entire set. The piece ends with a restatement of the syncopated theme of the opening. It is comprised of 11 dreams and is 2:50 minutes long.

---

[1] See figure 4.3, p. 21

Four of Wands

In the Waite deck, there is a great garland suspended from the four great staves planted in the foreground; two female figures uplift nosegays, and at their side is an arched entrance leading to an old manorial house. Waite associates this card with "country life, repose, concord, harmony, prosperity, peace, and the perfected work of these." Case also has "perfected work." In the Pholarcos deck, a lunar feminine figure and a masculine solar figure stand side by side, holding hands, and they have created four dragons with eyes in their tails and flames issuing from their mouths, celebrating completion. Two pairs of acrobats perform above. Sorrenti states, "Sun and Moon unite in the alchemical wedding. An aggregation of marimbas murmur music from every age, in a tag game of crescendos that chase each other through the delighted crowds. Time to celebrate." Common dream themes include female figures (6), male figures (4), bedrooms (2), and texts (2); concern (2) was a common emotion.

This piece is also in 4/4 time throughout, Allegro, and is scored for horn, Bb trumpet, trombone, and euphonium (no marimbas!). It opens with a statement of the Three of Wands tune in the trombone, followed by two variations and a restatement of the tune in the euphonium, followed by the horn, each time with figured accompaniments in the other instruments. This is followed by a new theme in the trumpet, with low interjections by the trombone, followed by the horn, with high interjections from the trumpet, and a final statement of the original theme by the three upper instruments. It is comprised of 8 dreams and is 3:30 minutes long.

Five of Wands

In the Waite deck, a posse of youths are brandishing staves, as if in sport or strife. Waite associates this card with "imitation, for example sham fight, the strenuous competition and struggle of the search after riches and fortune . . . gold, gain, opulence." Case has "strife, competition". In the Pholarcos deck, a man and a woman are dancing a vigorous tango, but they disagree on which direction to turn, while serpents and frogs are below. Sorrenti states, "The central frog holds the gang together despite the altercation – a mercurial overseer of operations. The fire will use your body as an alembic; contain the kindling of great heat, let it change you. This forging takes you to fertile territory where your creative children can be born." Common dream themes include male figures (5), groups (4), vehicles (3), money (2), trial (2), court (2), conflict (2), and archaeology (2). Concern (2) was a common emotion.

This tune is in 6/8 time throughout, and is scored for horn, Bb trumpet, trombone, and tuba. It begins very slowly, Lento, with a set of runs for horn, followed by trumpet. It then settles into a jig tune, Molto Vivace, which forms the basis of a rondo in which the trumpet has the lead. This is eventually taken over by the horn. There is an excursion, again led by the trumpet, after which the jig tune returns on the horn, followed by the trumpet. Another excursion follows, again led by the horn followed by the trumpet, and a final restatement of the jig tune on both horn and trumpet. The piece is comprised of 8 dreams, and is 3:45 minutes long.

Six of Wands

In the Waite deck, a laureled horseman bears a staff adorned with a laurel crown; footmen with staves are at his side. Waite associates this card with "a victor triumphing . . . great news . . . expectation crowned with its own desire, the crown of hope." Case has "victory after strife, gain." In the Pholarcos deck, a boy rides a horse towards the finish line, with alchemical symbols and the Saturn-Moon-Sun spiral above. Sorrenti states, "Jump through the hoop and another and another . . . the air glitters with victory . . . a gift of fire!" Common dream themes include male figures (5), female figures (3), conferences (2), and the colors red (2), black (2), and green (2). Surprise (2) was a common emotion.

This piece is in 4/4 time throughout, Molto Allegro, and is scored for horn, Bb trumpet, trombone, tuba, and snare drum. It opens with a rapid octave run up and down the scale for tuba, which will be thematic throughout the piece, with a snare drum rhythm beneath. On top of this, a theme is played on the horn. This is followed by another theme, first on trumpet, and then on horn, trombone, and tuba. Several other themes weave in and around this. The piece ends with the scale run on all the brass instruments. It consists of 9 dreams and is 3:00 minutes long.

Seven of Wands

In the Waite deck, a young man stands on a craggy eminence, brandishing a staff; six other staves are raised towards him from below. Waite associates this card with "valor . . . the vantage position . . . discussion, wordy strife . . . negotiations, war of trade, barter, competition . . . success." Case has "valor, courage in the face of difficulties." In the Pholarcos deck, a fiery female magician in a flaming dress, Artemisia, emanates sparks from her hands, and the words "ready . . . go!" are on banners above. The symbols for the fire signs (Aries, Leo, and Sagittarius) are tattooed on her left arm. An artemisia plant grows in a flourish from her head. Sorrenti states, "The rising fire of visionary action in the world. Mighty energies taking shape . . . her flame is strong enough that none can put her out." Common dream themes include music (3), home (2), trumpets (2), and practicing (2). Gladness (2) is a common emotion.

This piece is in 4/4 time throughout, Allegro, and is scored for horn, two Bb trumpets, trombone, and snare drum. It opens with a muted, slightly sardonic fanfare on trumpet, followed by the same figure on muted trombone. This leads to a simple declarative rondo theme on trumpet which is taken up by the trombone, with a syncopated overlay in the other instruments and a consistent underlay of rhythm provided by the drum. An excursion of dotted eighth and sixteenth note rhythm follows, followed by the declarative rondo theme. A second excursion follows, and the piece ends with a restatement of the rondo theme, and a kind of mock coda with a persistent 1:5:1 chord structure. The piece is comprised of 11 dreams, and is 3:05 minutes in length.

Eight of Wands

In the Waite deck, there is a flight of eight wands through an open country. Waite associates this card with "activity in undertakings, the path of such activity, swiftness, as that of an express messenger, great haste, great hope, speed towards an end which promises assured felicity, that which is on the move, also the arrows of love." Case has "activity, swiftness, approach to goal." In the Pholarcos deck, the tiger-footed figure of Mercurius, with the words "argento vivo" (living silver) and a Mercury symbol emblazoned on his shirt, bends backwards. A tiger cub follows. Its tail evaporates into a composite figure of a woman and a dragon. Above, an inverted acrobat with legs in the Aquarius position is flanked by another Mercury symbol and by the head of a woman whose crown is a rooster. Sorrenti states, "Every ally comes to the fire pit as you leap into the center; the quicksilver of Mercurius requires your molecules to dance with the rest of creation. Help is always at hand, do you recognize it?" Common dream themes include groups of people (5), airports (3), rivers (2), stone (2), and home (2). Success/victory (3) was a common emotion.

This piece is also in 4/4 time throughout, and is scored for horn, Bb trumpet, and trombone, Allegro Molto. It begins with a straightforward theme on the trumpet, followed by the horn and then by the trombone, and then the trumpet again. There is a lengthy excursion begun by the trumpet, followed by the horn. This goes through several further themes before returning to the original theme on the three instruments in succession as before. It is comprised of 8 dreams and is 2:50 minutes long.

Nine of Wands

In the Waite deck, a figure leans upon his staff and has an expectant look, as if awaiting an enemy. Behind him are eight other staves erect, in orderly disposition, like a palisade. Waite associates this card with "strength in opposition . . . delay, suspension, adjournment." Case has "preparedness, strength in reserve, victory after opposition." In the Pholarcos deck, a male figure dances within an oval (all of the Nines in this deck appear in ovals), the lower half of which is in flames, with a small horse-dragon at the bottom and a pair of lizards at the top. The eye in his heart opens to heaven. Sorrenti states, "The ecstatic still point where an essential quality is discovered and can be rooted in the heart. The visionary heart opens its eye, this is your dazzling initiation. Celebrate the surge of potency that maps meaning." Common dream themes include writing (3), lucidity (2), cars (2), my son (2), weapons (2), and the color red (2). Success (2) was a common emotion.

This piece is also in 4/4 time throughout, and is scored for horn, Bb trumpet, trombone, and euphonium, Moderato. It opens with a fanfare in C majorstarting on the trumpet and bringing in the other instruments. This is followed by a theme for the horn in A minor, with ascending and descending scales for the trumpet, repeated by the euphonium, with ascending and descending scales for the trombone. Another theme, still in A minor, is played on the trumpet, joined by the horn, and a third theme follows. There is a transition to a new theme in what is effectively G minor, but without a key signature change, followed by a transition to yet another theme in C major. This leads to a restatement of the original A minor theme. The piece is comprised of 11 dreams, and is 3:10 minutes in length.

Ten of Wands

In the Waite deck, a man is oppressed by the weight of the ten staves which he is carrying. Waite associates this card with "oppression simply, but it is also fortune, gain, any kind of success . . . false-seeming, disguise, perfidy." Case has "oppression, burden of ill-regulated power." In the Pholarcos deck, an unblindfolded man with green eyes, with a single white spirit horse on his headband, stares forwards, while two dragons similar to the one in the Nine of Wands are below. The words "lucid fire" appear below. Sorrenti states, "A fire can burn too high, too wide, too long – take time out, unburden." Common dream themes include female figures (5), death (3), negative male authority figures (3), positive male figures (3), children (3), Jews (2), conferences (2), computers (2), laws (2), conflict (2), and the colors blue (3), red (2), and yellow (2). Common emotions included concern (2) and interruption/intrusion (2).

This piece begins in 4/4 time, Allegro, and is scored for horn, Bb trumpet, trombone, tuba, triangle, and maracas. The horn sets up a syncopated rhythm at the beginning, underlain by a persistent maraca beat, and the trumpet comes in with rapid ascending and descending figures. These continue with themes played against them in the horn and trombone. This leads to a 3/4 section with a theme at first led by the trumpet, but picked up by the horn and trombone. There is an aria-like theme in the trombone. This leads to a section in 6/8 time, with a horn-trombone duet which becomes a horn-trumpet duet. Further new thematic material is introduced, mostly for trumpet or trombone, leading to a conclusion. The piece is comprised of 14 dreams, and its length is 4:15 minutes.

King of Wands

In the Waite deck, there is a king enthroned, with a flowering wand. A lion is emblazoned on the back of his throne. Waite associates this card with a "dark man, friendly, countryman, generally married, honest, conscientious." Case has "dark man, friendly, ardent, honesty, possible inheritance." In the Pholarcos deck, the king is a dark-skinned man, with a dragon crown inscribed with the letter M. A chiseled dragon-horse adorns his collar. Sorrenti states, "A book exists to look up quests and motivation. A golden nugget falls out, inscribed with equations for daily alchemy. The current in the room is staggering." There were no common dream themes. Common dream emotions included judgment/decision/balance (3).

This piece is in 4/4 time throughout, Moderato, and is scored for the largest ensemble in the Wands section: two horns, Bb trumpet, trombone, euphonium, tuba, cymbals, snare drum, and bass drum. Similar to the Seven of Wands, it opens with a somewhat sarcastic, muted call on the trumpet, followed by a similar muted call on the trombone. This leads to a royal fanfare starting on the euphonium and tuba, then picked up the horns, and then, with ornamentation, by the trombone and tuba, followed again by the trumpet and horn. While the trumpet repeats the fanfare theme, the low brass instruments interrupt with a new theme. This is followed by a section for the horns, underlain by syncopated rhythm in the trombone, tuba, and snare drum. This is picked up by the trombone and tuba, while the horns have the syncopated rhythm. The trumpet takes it up, followed by the euphonium. A new theme emerges on the trombone, picked up by the trumpet. This leads to a repeat of the fanfare theme on the horns and trumpet, again underlain by the interrupting theme on all three of the lower instruments. The piece concludes with some ascending and descending scales for all the brass instruments. It is comprised of 7 dreams, and its length is 2:35 minutes.

Queen of Wands

In the Waite deck, there is a queen enthroned. Waite associates this card with a "dark woman or countrywoman, friendly, chaste, loving, honorable." Case has "dark woman, magnetic, friendly, business success." In the Pholarcos deck, there is an oval-faced female figure with her hair aflame. There appears to be an open book below, with a small golden dragon on its spine. Sorrenti states, "Her face is criss-crossed with rich mineral ore from the heart-cave. A blue spray of rain is visible through her molten lava hair. She sits on the throne and fingers the fulgid wee dragon that lives in her heart chamber till they both cast the velvet green of their eyes upon you. Your turn to unleash enchantment, the crazy magnetism of creativity." Common dream themes include male figures (4), female figures (3), death (3), data (2), and the color black (2). Mourning (2) was a common emotion.

This piece is scored for horn, Bb trumpet, trombone, euphonium, and tuba, and it opens with a fanfare in 4/4 time, Allegro, for trumpet and horn, with descending scales on the euphonium. This is followed by a 3/4 section, an extended series of graceful waltz tunes mostly carried by the horn, trumpet, and trombone, and occasionally by the tuba and euphonium. The piece is comprised of 13 dreams, and its length is 5:00 minutes.

Knight of Wands

In the Waite deck, a horseman is shown as if upon a journey, armed with a short wand. Although he is in full armor, he is not on a warlike errand. Waite associates this card with "departure, absence, flight, emigration. A dark young man." Case has "dark, friendly young man, departure, change of residence." In the Pholarcos deck, a young female figure looks upwards, while a white fox transforms out of the fire in her chest. Sorrenti states, "This Anubis-like presence is ready to guide any essential quest. Just step through the small portal and meet the psychopomps who will ferry your journeys back and forth between the worlds . . . In fire, you will be led to unpredictable vision, salves of meaning, adventure." This was the first card I drew at the 2021 Tarot workshop, relating to past completed projects[2]. Common dream themes include male figures (5), rooms (3), dwellings (3), numbers (2), cards (2), music (2), passages (2), and the color red (3). The emotion of uncertainty (2) was present.

This piece is scored for Bb trumpet and trombone. It opens in 3/4 time, Allegro, with a rondo theme which features dotted eighth note and sixteenth note rhythms, which mimic the pace of the horse on which the knight rides. There is an excursion into a more waltz-like section, followed by the rondo theme. A second excursion in 4/4 time has a lively theme for both instruments. The piece ends with a restatement of the rondo theme. It is comprised of 11 dreams, and is 3:40 minutes long.

Page of Wands

In the Waite deck, a young man stands in the act of proclamation. He is unknown but faithful, and his tidings are strange. Waite associates this card with a "dark young man, faithful, a lover, an envoy, a postman." Case has "a dark young man, messenger, brilliance, courage." In the Pholarcos deck, a woman with flaming red hair looks downwards. Sorrenti states, "The dreamer stands on the verge of becoming, a steep cliff where visions take shape. A small whirlwind starts at ground level, sweeping round the furniture." Common dream themes were male figures (5), houses (3), and female figures (2). Surprise (2) was a common emotion.

---

[2] See figure 4.3, p. 21.

The last of the Wands pieces is in 4/4 time throughout, Allegretto, and is scored for horn, Bb trumpet, trombone, and harmonium. For the most part, the harmonium provides chordal underlays and arpeggios, while the melodies are in the brass instruments. There is a single, very simple theme on trumpet which opens the piece and which is heard throughout the piece on each of the brass instruments in turn, while the other instruments play variations upon it. The piece is comprised of 6 dreams, and its length is 2:25 minutes.

✦ 10 ✦
The Minor Arcana – Cups

There were a total of 91 dreams associated with Cups: 71 with dream text, 12 without dream text, and 8 duplicates. All three of the possible musical keys for the Water element (G, Eb, and B major and their relative minors) were used for these compositions. Altogether, the fourteen Cups pieces are 45:35 minutes in length.

Ace of Cups

In the Waite deck, a hand issues from a cloud, holding in its palm a cup, from which five streams are pouring into the sea. Waite associates this card with "true heart, joy, contentment, abode, nourishment, abundance." Case has "fertility, productiveness, beauty, pleasure." In the Pholarcos deck, a hoodwinked woman, under water, has coral and anemones growing out of the top of her head, while jellyfish float to her right. Sorrenti states, "This place is teeming with sacred life and longing: the longing for connection, tendrils reaching in all directions . . . tides submerge you in emotion, the depths of connection, the unconscious . . . Lap in nurturance, mystery, union." Common dream themes include female figures (3), groups (3), male figures (2), meetings (2), and songs (2). Common emotions include concern (2) and hope (2).

This piece is in 4/4 time throughout, in G major, Moderato. It is scored for violin, cello, and guitar. It opens with a gentle theme on guitar which is picked up in turn by the cello and then by the violin. A second theme is played first on violin, then on cello, then on guitar, followed by a repeat of the original theme on guitar with variations in the violin and cello. Another excursion follows on the second theme on violin, then on cello, with guitar variations. A final statement of the original theme on all three instruments follows, with a brief, energetic coda. The piece is comprised of 6 dreams, and its length is 3:50 minutes.

Two of Cups

In the Waite deck, a youth and maiden are pledging to one another. Above their cups rises the caduceus of Hermes. Waite associates this card with "love, passion, friendship, affinity, union, concord, sexual relations." Case has "reciprocity, reflection." In the Pholarcos deck, there is an underwater scene of two large coral branches reaching out to one another, while two fish swim between them and jellyfish are above. In the upper right corner, a partial circle contains the spiral with the symbols for Saturn, Sun, and Moon in a vertical row, while a crab extends its claws into the periphery. Sorrenti states, "The deep sea heart is pulsing – it fills the coral and ripples into the water as story and life. The contact is made. The sea roars through your chest. Some call it the mystery of substance, attraction. This thing of rapture that ignites the lights at the bottom of the sea." Common dream themes include female figures (4), music (3), garments (2), repairs (2), and the colors brown (2) and yellow (2).

This piece, in E minor with occasional excursions into G major, is in 3/4 time throughout. It is scored for string trio (violin, viola, and cello), Andantino. It begins with a ground set up by the cello, above which a series of slightly sad waltz tunes is played on violin, with accompaniment by the viola above the cello ground. The viola and cello take the lead in some places, and the cello has the original waltz tune at the close. The piece is comprised of 7 dreams, and its length is 4:05 minutes.

Three of Cups

In the Waite deck, three maidens in a garden celebrate with cups uplifted, as if pledging to one another. Waite associates this card with "the conclusion of any matter, plenty, perfection, merriment, happiness, victory, fulfillment, solace, healing." Case has "pleasure, liberality, fulfillment, happy issue." In the Pholarcos deck, a female accordionist plays at the bottom of the sea; a male drummer plays above and sings to the Moon; and a pregnant woman dances with three dragonflies in the middle, apparently on the surface of the water. Sorrenti states, "Music kissing us into shape, the deep well of love spreading like butter on every surface, no order left, just the glory of expansion, friendship, sharing." Music (2) is the only common dream theme.

This piece, in G major, is in 4/4 time throughout, Andante. It is scored for string trio. The cello introduces a short theme, which is followed in canon by the viola and then by the violin. A variation on the same tune is then played, again canonically by the violin, viola, and cello, and after a stretto passage on ascending scales the original tune is played by all three instruments in unison. This is followed by a section on staccato eighth notes in ascending and descending figures, tossed back and forth among the three instruments. A third section begins with a new tune on the violin, played in canon by the viola and then by the cello, followed by a unison statement of the theme on all three instruments. The piece ends with a unison restatement of the original theme. The piece is comprised of 5 dreams and is 2:25 minutes long.

Four of Cups

In the Waite deck, a young man seated under a tree contemplates three cups set on the grass before him. He expresses discontent with his environment. A hand issuing from a cloud offers him another cup. Waite associates this card with "weariness, disgust, aversion, imaginary vexations . . . no consolation . . . blended pleasure." Case has "contemplation, dissatisfaction with material success." In the Pholarcos deck, a female circus acrobat sits at the base of a tree which extends under the water, in which four turtles are swimming. She turns away from them. A series of four cups falls out of the Moon. A rainbow extends from the surface of the water up to the tree. Sorrenti states, "Bored of so much beauty, you may prefer to just keep your feet up, keep your clothes on, look away. Still they will come at you, generous eyes, cheery grins." Common dream themes include male figures (3), dwellings (2), female figures (2), and the number 4 (2).

This piece is in C minor, and is in 4/4 time throughout, Molto Vivace. It is scored for a string quartet (two violins, viola, and cello), and it is a four-voiced fugue, each of its voices deriving from one dream. Its composition was inspired by the long, detailed dream presented in Chapter Five[1]. The first fugue subject (A), a rapid ascending and descending figure, is introduced by the cello, followed by the viola, followed by each of the violins in turn. While the first violin is playing it, the cello introduces the second theme (B), a slower, descending figure. This is similarly picked up by the viola and the violins in turn. While the second violin is playing it, the cello introduces the third theme (C), a very rapid ascending and descending figure. This is picked up by the viola and then by the second violin while the first violin is playing theme B. The cello introduces the fourth theme (D)[2] under the second violin's statement of theme C, and it is picked up by the viola under the first violin's statement of theme C. Theme D is then picked up by the second violin, followed by the first violin. This leads to restatement of theme A on the cello and viola, followed by the first violin, while the second violin plays theme B. Theme B is picked up by the first violin while the cello repeats theme A, the second violin plays theme C, and the cello plays theme D. The viola then picks up theme B while the first violin plays theme C. While this is in progress, the cello picks up theme B while the viola plays theme C. Then the first violin repeats theme A while the cello plays theme C. Both violins play theme A in canon, followed by the second violin and viola, followed by the viola and cello, while the first violin, and then the second violin, restate theme C, followed by a restatement of theme D in the first violin. The piece ends with a unison restatement of theme B. The piece is 2:30 minutes long.

---

[1] See supra, pp. 29-30.
[2] See supra, p.22.

Five of Cups

In the Waite deck, a dark, cloaked figure looks at three prone cups; two other cups stand upright behind him. A bridge is in the background. Waite associates this card with "loss, but something remains . . . inheritance, transmission, and patrimony." Case has "loss in pleasure, partial loss, vain regret." In the Pholarcos deck, a female violinist with a jellyfish body, whose left arm is made up of five jellyfish, plays before a towering wave. Sorrenti states, "The loneliness is excruciating. Wailing womb, wailing water, wailing *wall*. This is the tearing of the heart. The sonatas will keep reverberating until every tear has found release. Water knows how to cleanse the hostage heart, gift it back to joy." Common dream themes include female figures (6), male leaders (4), vehicles (4), violent death (3), young men (3), cities (2), and the color black (2).

This piece, in G major, begins in 4/4 time, Allegretto. It is scored for string trio. The violin states a graceful rondo theme, underlain by pizzicato arpeggios on the cello. The tune is picked up by the viola, with pizzicato arpeggios on the violin. A canonical section for all three instruments, played arco, follows, with syncopated notes. This is followed by a restatement of the rondo theme on the cello, with pizzicato arpeggios on the viola. There is a brief section in which first the cello, then the violin play descending scales against pizzicato arpeggios on the other instruments. A new theme is taken up by the viola, followed by the violin and then by the cello, with the syncopated underlay from the canonical section on the viola. This leads to an excursion into 3/4 time with a new theme for the violin, while the viola continues the syncopated underlay. A new theme, still in 3/4, is played by the violin while the cello takes up the syncopations. This leads to a restatement of the rondo theme in 4/4 time on the violin, with the pizzicato arpeggios on the cello. The piece concludes with a coda on a 1-5-1-5-1 chordal structure, played by all three instruments. The piece is comprised of 9 dreams, and is 4:05 minutes in length.

Six of Cups

In the Waite deck, two children are in an old garden, their cups filled with flowers. Waite associates this card with "memories and the past . . . reflecting on childhood, happiness, enjoyment, new relations, new environment, new knowledge." Case has "beginning of steady gain, but beginning only, new relations, new environment." In the Pholarcos deck, a magician with a red ball for a nose hands another red ball to a child with a similar ball at her heart. They are supported by a large cup surrounded by vegetation. The Saturn-Moon-Sun spiral, above, is associated with the words "incarnation . . . essential quest . . . Soul song map", while an alembic containing the lunar crescent accompanied by the words "cooking soul" is approached by a scorpion. Sorrenti states, "She plays at the beach shack, carries in a large bowl of silver liquid for you to wash your face. She then announces with such glee about the moon and all her magic – and she knows you know . . . a gift of water." The only common dream theme was the presence of male figures (2).

This piece is in B major, Allegro, and is scored for string trio. It begins with a rapid descending theme in 4/4 time on violin, while the other two instruments play syncopated quarter-half-quarter notes. This is theme picked up, in turn, by the cello and then by the viola. The viola then introduces a new theme, underlain by the syncopations in the other two instruments. This is repeated by the violin, and then by the cello. The time signature changes to 6/8, with a new theme for the viola, underlain by the syncopations. The original theme returns in 4/4, again picked up by the cello and then by the viola. The piece is comprised of 4 dreams, and is 3:30 minutes long.

Seven of Cups

In the Waite deck, there are strange chalices of vision. Waite associates this card with "Fairy favors, images of reflection, imagination, sentiment . . . contemplation, some attainment . . . but nothing permanent or substantial." Case has "illusionary success, ideas, designs, resolutions." In the Pholarcos deck, the central figure is a woman inside a watery oval or mirror, in which a single electric bulb is shown lit. The top of the oval is sealed by a pair of angel fish. At the bottom are seven chalices, from two of which emerge vapors supporting bulbs upon which a man and a woman stand. An eagle is perched below the oval, while an owl flies above. The words "hear soul requirements" are written below the oval. Sorrenti states, "You are watching a new birth and it is not fantasy but your *imaginatio vera*. Among heaps of curios, here is a choice dictated by your soul requirements." Common dream themes include female figures (3), male figures (3), and regimes (2). Common emotions include oppression (2) and escape (2).

This piece, in Eb major, is in 3/4 time throughout. It is scored for string trio, Allegretto. It opens with an arpeggio theme, pizzicato, on the violin. This is picked up by the viola, with a countermelody on the cello. It is restated by the violin, with a different countermelody on the viola. The viola then takes up the melody with the same countermelody on the cello; then the violin takes up the countermelody with a different countermelody on the cello. The viola introduces another new melody. This is followed by a restatement of the original melody on violin and viola, in unison, a fifth apart. The viola continues the original melody against the first countermelody on the cello. The piece is comprised of 5 dreams, and its length is 3:45 minutes.

Eight of Cups

In the Waite deck, a man of dejected aspect is deserting the cups of his felicity, enterprise, undertaking or previous concern. Waite associates this card with "joy, mildness, timidity, honor, modesty." Case has "abandoned success, instability, leaving material success for something higher." In the Pholarcos deck, there is an image of a man with a cat perched on his head, submerged in water up to his chest, in a mountainous region. Eight chalices are below, four beneath and four above the surface of the water. Sorrenti states, "There are trees along the edge. Far below, the sea pulses with myriad green undertones of water plants." Common dream themes include restaurants (2), female figures (2), destruction of written material (2), and the colors black (2) and yellow-green/olive green (2). Decisiveness (2) was a common emotion.

This piece is in G major, Moderato, and is scored for string trio. It begins with a waltz tune in 3/4 time for the violin, while the other instruments play pizzicato accompaniments. This is then taken up by the cello, with the pizzicatos above. A new pair of themes is introduced on the violin, arco, and by the cello, pizzicato. The violin tune ends in a series of rapidly ascending and descending scales. These are taken up by the viola, and this leads to a restatement of the original theme on violin, with pizzicato accompaniment as before. This leads to a section in 6/8 time, with a new melody tossed back and forth among the three instruments, sometimes pizzicato, sometimes arco. The piece concludes in 3/4 time with a restatement in unison of the rapidly ascending and descending scales. The piece is comprised of 8 dreams, and its length is 4:15 minutes.

Nine of Cups

In the Waite deck, a goodly personage is feasting to his heart's content, and a refreshment of wine is in the nine cups on the arched counter behind him. Waite associates this card with "concord, physical bien-etre, also victory, success, advantage, satisfaction." Case has "material success, physical well-being." In the Pholarcos deck, nine orcas sport in the water, with mountains in the background, overseen by a Full Moon and a large eye. A canoe carries a pair of people and a harp, with the words "dreams and emotion in motion" written on it. Below, a pregnant woman gives birth to nine dragonflies from her throat. The words "the whale comes on shore to look with your eye – dreams will love you to completion" emerge as if from her womb. Sorrenti states, "Music opens the hearts of this great gathering. The carnival of your best wish unfolds across the hills. Dreams do love us to completion." Common dream themes include food items (2) and male figures (2).

This piece is in C minor, and is in 3/4 time throughout, Moderato. It is scored for string quartet. It begins with a forcefully stated phrase in the cello, picked up by the other instruments. A steady quarter note beat continues throughout the piece, traded off among the instruments, usually played arco, but played pizzicato in one section. The rest of the thematic material is tightly interwoven, so it is not easy to pick apart themes, but the opening phrase repeats at the end. The piece is comprised of 4 themes, and is 4:10 minutes long.

Ten of Cups

In the Waite deck, an apparition of ten cups in a rainbow is contemplated in wonder and ecstasy by a man and woman below. Two children dancing near them have not observed this prodigy. Waite associates this card with "contentment, repose of the entire heart." Case has "lasting success, happiness to come." In the Pholarcos deck, there is an unblindfolded female figure with a branch of coral running up the bridge of her nose and branching to the left. Mermaids swim up and down her cheeks. A series of ten jellyfish bearing chalices is below, along with a descending serpent and an ascending dragonfly. Sorrenti states, "She feels the interconnection between all things, as with Pisces. Love fulfills itself and is felt to the very center of the beating heart and out through all things. The dream poet whispers that 1 and 10 are rituals of height and descent – the one and the ten thousand things – and the other numbers, the enthusiasm to fully live." Common dream themes include female figures (3), children (3), teachers (2), houses (2), lunch (2), and music (2). Observation (2) is a common emotion.

This piece is in G major, and is scored for violin, viola, cello, and double bass. It begins, Allegro, in 4/4 time with a melody in the violin matched in inversion in the viola, with syncopated accompaniment in the lower two instruments. This leads to a section in 3/4 time whose thematic material consists of a declarative short opening statement (at first on the cello, but taken up later by the other instruments in turn) to which there is a short, somewhat argumentative response (at first on the violin, but also taken up later by the other instruments in turn). This is followed by a waltz tune played first on the violin, while the double bass resumes the syncopated underlay. The cello takes up the waltz tune, with the syncopated underlay on the viola. This is followed by a restatement of the declaration-and-response. It leads to a section in 4/4 time which introduces a new theme, first on the violin, then on the viola, while first the viola and the cello, and then the violin and double bass, play triplets, pizzicato, below it. The time signature returns to 3/4 for a restatement of the declaration-and-response, then back to 4/4 for a new, syncopated theme on the violin, below which the response is played, in duple time, by the other instruments in turn. The piece closes with a restatement of the opening theme and accompaniment. The piece is comprised of 8 dreams, and its length is 2:45 minutes.

King of Cups

In the Waite deck, an enthroned king holds a short scepter in his left hand and a great cup in his right. His throne is set upon the sea. Waite associates this card with a "fair man, man of business, law, or divinity, responsible." Case has "fair man, calm exterior, subtle, violent, artistic." In the Pholarcos deck, the King is fair-skinned and bears a crown of coral. A turtle swims below, and another crowned figure in a robe appears to be petitioning the King. Sorrenti states, "The king's inner poet is at work, raising a bowl to his lips which color when he considers how to address his kingdom. The poetry is gathered in the bowl for further refinement . . . Over time, a cluster of coral in the Aegean Sea turned into the shape of a man. He felt lonely and warbled soft songs to all fins swimming by. He could feel who was coming at great distances, the shape of their hearts on that day. He would sing accordingly and it filled travelers with such intensity that the excess rushed into waves of vivid dreaming and changing colors. All that sea-green of lore, the king must be singing." Common dream themes include female figures (3), male figures (2), family groups (2), and the colors red (2) and yellow (2).

This piece is in B major, Allegro, and is scored for string trio. It begins in 3/4 time with a fanfare, building up from the cello to the viola to the violin. This is followed by a waltz tune played in canonical thirds, first by the violin, then by the cello, then by the viola, then again by the violin and the cello. This leads to another waltz tune on the viola, followed by the violin. This is followed by a section of dotted eighth and sixteenth note rhythms tossed back and forth among the instruments. This leads to a brief section in 6/8 time, with another melody tossed back and forth among the instruments, followed by the original waltz tune, but this time starting in the cello followed by the viola, followed by the violin. The piece is comprised of 5 dreams, and its length is 3:25 minutes.

Queen of Cups

In the Waite deck, a beautiful, fair, dreamy enthroned queen sees visions in her cup. Waite associates this card with a "good, fair woman, honest, devoted . . . loving intelligence, and hence the gift of vision, success, happiness, pleasure, also wisdom." Case has "fair woman, imaginative, poetic, gift of vision." In the Pholarcos deck, the Queen is a dark-haired young woman who holds a white panther and a chalice in her lap. A single coral bloom emerges from her hair, while a branching coral surrounds her head. Water pours from her sleeve. Sorrenti states, "The whole vast sea is reaching endlessly as if stretching out for you to run across the world. And she is here, she is always here, her eyes the intimate enclosure where whales mate – even the most feral of creatures will sit still upon her lap, flick a seductive tail, flex its longing. Master the internal shimmering." Common dream themes include music (3) and female figures (3). Violent combat (2) is a common emotion.

This piece is in G major and is a duet for violin and cello, Allegretto, in 4/4 time throughout. The violin opens with a theme, which is picked up in canon by the cello. The cello continues the theme while the violin plays a descending series of eighth notes over it. The violin continues with a slightly ornamented version of the theme, while the cello has the eighth note accompaniment. This continues while the violin plays a new theme, which is then picked up by the cello in canon. This is followed by the violin proposing a short new theme, on which the cello comments rhythmically. Then their roles are reversed. This leads to a restatement of the original theme in the violin, again followed by the cello in canon. The piece is comprised of 7 dreams, and is 3:10 minutes long.

Knight of Cups

In the Waite deck, a graceful, not warlike horseman rides quietly, wearing a winged helmet. Waite associates this card with "arrival, approach — sometimes that of a messenger, advances, proposition, demeanor, invitation, incitement." Case has "fair man, Venusian, indolent, arrival, approach." In the Pholarcos deck, there is a young woman with luxuriant hair under the Full Moon, with descending and ascending birds riding her arms, while two horses emerge from the sides. Sorrenti states, "In water you will be led to exploration of the depths, sublime or illusory love, beauty." Common dream themes include male figures (4), food (3), groups (2), grass (2), open areas (2), and the color green (2).

This piece is in G major, and is scored for string trio, Allegretto. It begins with a waltz tune in 3/4 time on the violin and viola, followed by a countermelody on the viola while the violin and cello play fragments of it in response. The cello continues the countermelody, while the violin and viola play pizzicato accompaniments over it. The viola introduces a new theme, arco, while the violin continues the pizzicato accompaniment and the cello introduces another new theme. Then the viola and cello trade places while the violin continues, pizzicato. This is followed by a section in 4/4 time. The viola states a new theme, while the violin has pizzicato arpeggios above it and the cello has eighth notes below. The violin picks up the theme, arco, while the cello has the pizzicato arpeggios and the viola has the eighth notes. The viola continues the pizzicato arpeggios while the violin introduces a new theme. This theme is then picked up by the viola, while the cello has the pizzicato arpeggios. This leads to a recapitulation of the original 3/4 waltz tune, followed by the countermelody with its fragments, as before. The piece is comprised of 7 dreams, and its length is 3:25 minutes.

Page of Cups

In the Waite deck, a fair, pleasing, somewhat effeminate Page, of studious intent, contemplates a fish rising from a cup he holds. Waite associates this card with a "fair young man . . . a studious youth, news, message, application, reflection, meditation – also those things directed to business." Case has "fair studious youth, reflection, news." In the Pholarcos deck, a red-haired woman kisses the brow of a cheetah. A large chalice containing a heart is surrounded by three whales. Sorrenti states, "She can feel when the waterfall is cut off and knows they have diverted its course for electricity." Common dream themes include young male figures (2) and organizing/orienting (2).

This piece is in G major, Moderato, and is a duet for violin and cello. It begins in 4/4 time with a simple theme on violin, with cello accompaniment. This is followed by a section in 3/4 time which features a series of countermelodies on violin and cello. The piece is comprised of 5 dreams, and is 2:50 minutes long.

◆ 11 ◆
The Minor Arcana – Swords

A total of 117 dreams were associated with Swords: 94 with dream text, 14 without dream text, and 9 duplicates. Although F# major could have been used for these compositions, in fact only the Air element keys D major and Bb major and their relative minors were used. Altogether, the fourteen Cups pieces are 47:35 minutes in length.

Ace of Swords

In the Waite deck, a hand issues from a cloud, grasping a sword, the point of which is encircled by a crown. Waite associates this card with "triumph, the excessive degree in everything, conquest . . . a card of great force, in love as well as in hatred." Case has "invoked force, conquest, activity." In the Pholarcos deck, there is a hoodwinked figure out of whose head emerges a proliferation of swallows, hummingbirds, cranes, songbirds, and birds of paradise. Sorrenti states, "that which develops mind, concept, communication . . . every potential on wings soaring through realms of consciousness, conceiving reality, tremoring into new idea, seeking wisdom." Common dream themes include holes in the ground (3), outdoor locations (2), archaeological sites (2), former students (2), and music (2).

This piece, in Bb major, is in 3/4 time throughout, Allegretto. It is scored for flute, oboe, and Bb clarinet. It opens with a waltz tune for clarinet, followed by a countermelody for all three instruments in close harmony. The flute picks up the original tune, with accompaniments in the other instruments. This is followed by an excursion led by the flute, with the clarinet playing a variation on the original tune and the oboe playing an accompaniment. The flute then picks up the original tune, joined by the oboe, while the clarinet plays an accompaniment. All three instruments then reprise the countermelody. The piece is comprised of 7 dreams, and is 3:05 minutes long.

Two of Swords

In the Waite deck, a hoodwinked female figure balances two swords upon her shoulders. Waite associates this card with "conformity and the equipoise which it suggests, courage, friendship, affection, concord in a state of arms, intimacy." Case has "balanced force, indecision, friendship." In the Pholarcos deck, two suspended alembics hold birds named "king" and "queen". Twin circus acrobats hang from the periphery of a half-circle above, which contains the Saturn – Sun – Moon spiral. A number of rods with balls at each end are in the air above, and the words "a circus act", "Alchemy of opposites," "light . . . dark", and the Mercury symbol accompanied by the words "messenger of every god" are written below. Sorrenti states, "The twins, flitting eyes tracking and translating inner vision, making opposites for fun, constructing language and naming things, and quarreling, debating, making noise. They form a language to communicate with each other despite opposing views." Common dream themes include groups (2) and campsites (2).

This piece, in D major, is in 3/4 time throughout, Allegretto. It is scored for woodwind quartet (flute, oboe, Bb clarinet, and bassoon). It opens with the three upper instruments playing countermelodies while the bassoon plays syncopated rhythms. The flute takes up a new melody, while the bassoon has a repeated figure of a triplet plus two quarter notes. This melody is taken up by the clarinet, while the oboe has the repeated figure. The flute takes up a new melody while the repeated figure is played on the clarinet, and the bassoon resumes the syncopated rhythm. The oboe takes up this melody, while the flute has the repeated rhythm and the clarinet plays the syncopations. The piece closes with the oboe taking the lead on the main countermelody, with the accompanying countermelodies on the other 3 instruments. The piece is comprised of 7 dreams, and its length is 2:40 minutes.

Three of Swords

In the Waite deck, three swords pierce a heart, with cloud and rain behind. Waite associates this card with "removal, absence, delay, division, rupture, dispersion." Case has "sorrow, disappointment, tears, delay, absence, separation." In the Pholarcos deck, a man in a falcon costume and crown is winging forward, while a female figure above emits three spirals of air from her mouth which transform into stars. An inverted acrobat with a dagger swings from a trapeze above. Sorrenti states, "The first great cries, words turned to daggers, frenzy. Balancing the act of becoming conscious, division creates what seems to be unbearable pain. Gather the seeds of its wisdom, the storm will blow over and the teachings will be etched within." Common dream themes include groups of people (3), male figures (3), vehicles (2), residences, (2) and detectives (2).

This piece is in Bb major, Allegretto. It is scored for flute, Bb clarinet, bassoon, triangle, and snare drum. It begins with a fanfare for flute in 3/4 time, followed by clarinet and bassoon in close thirds, the rhythm of which is also in the snare drum. The fanfare continues into a section in 4/4 time on the flute and drum, now joined by the triangle at the downbeat of each measure, while the clarinet plays a melody with a countermelody on the bassoon. This melody is picked up by the flute, while the countermelody is played on the clarinet and the fanfare rhythm by the bassoon and drum. Then the melody is played by the bassoon, while the fanfare rhythm is played by the clarinet and the countermelody is played on the flute and drum. The flute and clarinet play a duet in thirds which is a variant of the melody, while the bassoon has the countermelody. The next section is introduced by the bassoon with a syncopated rhythm, over which the clarinet comes in with a similar melody – the drum drops out for this section. This is followed by a lively new melody on the bassoon, followed by the clarinet and the flute, while the drum resumes the fanfare rhythm. The triangle drops out for this section, but returns in the next, brief section in 2/4 time with 3 countermelodies in the wind instruments. These continue into the following 4/4 section. This leads to a section in 6/8, with first the flute, then the clarinet playing a new theme with sixteenth note triplets against a rhythmic theme, first in the clarinet and then in the oboe, as well as the drum. The piece concludes with a restatement of the original theme in the clarinet with the fanfare on the flute and drum and the countermelody on the bassoon, followed by a statement of the original theme on all three wind instruments. The piece is comprised of 9 dreams, and is 4:25 minutes long.

Four of Swords

In the Waite deck, there is an effigy of a knight in the attitude of prayer, lying at full length upon his tomb. Waite associates this card with "vigilance, retreat, solitude, hermit's repose, exile, tomb and coffin." Case has "rest from strife, relief from anxiety, quietness, rest, rest after illness." In the Pholarcos deck, a male dancer is being birthed within a circle; he extends arms, which end in daggers, beyond the periphery, while a coil around both of his arms has arrows at both ends. Below the circle is an eye, a Venus symbol plus a Mercury symbol, from which a kundalini serpent extends to the man's heart center. The words "remember from whence you have come . . . respect the great invisibles" are written below. Sorrenti states, "the eye of the storm, a still point for revelation, an ear for the wind . . . be still as fragments swirl round you, light up at neck level, chant a message through your lips. Rituals make heart grooves so the ledge of tears turns to soaring raven." Female figures (2) were the only common dream themes.

This piece in Bb major begins in 4/4 time, Andante. It is scored for woodwind quartet. It begins with the bassoon setting up a simple rhythmic figure, which carries through most of the piece. The oboe comes in above this with another simple rhythmic melody. Then the flute comes in with a more complicated melody, followed by an even more complicated melody on the clarinet. This is followed by a section in which all four melodies are played together. The final section is in 3/2 time, with long sixteenth note runs on the flute while the oboe plays a slower version of its theme and the clarinet and bassoon play a more lyrical variant of the clarinet melody. The piece is comprised of only 2 dreams, and is 2:35 minutes long.

Five of Swords

In the Waite deck, a disdainful man looks after two retreating and dejected figures. Their two swords lie upon the ground. He carries two others on his left shoulder, and a third sword is in his right hand, pointing to earth. Waite associates this card with "degradation, destruction, reversal, infamy, dishonor, loss." Case has "defeat, loss, failure, slander, dishonor." In the Pholarcos deck, the figure of a blonde woman made of glass has dagger points emerging from her ears, while third pierces her heart and two more are aimed at her from above at her head. A white hummingbird is consuming her heart, which is within an alembic. The words "and so we bleed" appear above. Sorrenti states, "How she bonds with new innocence . . . do not let the mind swallow up the heart." Common dream themes include family members (3), food (2), employment (2), containers (3), dreams (2), and music (2).

This piece is in D major, Andante, and is in 4/4 time, throughout. It is scored for wind quartet. It opens with a noble rondo theme on the oboe, followed by a countermelody on the bassoon. The oboe and bassoon then play the rondo theme together, an octave apart. This is followed by an excursion on a new pair of themes on the flute and clarinet, which are then picked up by the oboe and bassoon. This is followed by a restatement of the rondo theme on flute and oboe, one octave apart. A second excursion introduces new themes on all four instruments. The rondo theme returns, on flute, followed by the countermelody on the oboe, and the piece ends with a restatement of the rondo theme on all four instruments in unison. The piece is comprised of 9 dreams, and is 4:55 minutes long.

Six of Swords

In the Waite deck, a ferryman is carrying passengers in his boat to the further shore. Waite associates this card with "a journey by water, route, way, envoy, commissionary, expedient." Case has "success after anxiety, passage from difficulties, a journey by water." In the Pholarcos deck, a boy with a red sphere at his heart stands upon the back of a flying falcon. Six coils of air float below. Above is the circle and the Saturn-Sun-Moon spiral, and the words "we have even made the sky! . . . joy unbound → revel". Sorrenti states, "The speed fills the sky and makes the boy feel free . . . The storm is behind now and the waves far below . . . a gift of air." Common dream themes include groups (3) and campsites (2). Help/advice (2) was a common emotion.

This piece is in D major, Moderato, and is scored for flute, Bb clarinet, bassoon, and hand cymbals. It opens in 3/4 time with a melody on flute, underlain by clarinet arpeggios, followed by bassoon arpeggios. A short countermelody follows on the clarinet, followed by the flute. The bassoon then takes up the original melody with arpeggios on the flute. The flute introduces a new, simple melody while the bassoon continues the arpeggios, followed by the clarinet. This leads to a section in 4/4 time, with a new melody introduced on the clarinet, followed by the flute. This leads to a section in which the clarinet plays a lively dance tune, accompanied by syncopated rhythms on the flute and bassoon. This tune is taken up by the flute, with the clarinet and bassoon playing syncopations. The flute introduces a new melody over the bassoon syncopations, which is then taken up by the clarinet. This leads to a final reprise, in 3/4 time, of the original melody on flute and bassoon, with clarinet arpeggios. The piece is comprised of 5 dreams, and is 4:30 minutes long.

Seven of Swords

In the Waite deck, a man is in the act of carrying away five swords rapidly, while two others remain stuck in the ground. Waite associates this card with "design, attempt, wish, hope, confidence, also quarrelling. A plan that may fail, annoyance." Case has "unstable effort, uncertainty, partial success." In the Pholarcos deck, an armless girl dressed like Lewis Carroll's Alice has seven feathers sprouting from her shoulders, which seven hummingbirds hovering around her are pulling out. A series of seven breath spirals is on the lower part of her dress. Sorrenti states, "They call him tricky, mercury is always so, leading you through endless maddening play. The mind is so . . . You are weaving your own wings, how will you use them?" Common dream themes include male figures (6), female figures (5), music (4), Italian food (2), the number 3 (2), yards (2), and archaeological sites (2).

This piece is in D major, Moderato, and is scored for flute, oboe, English horn, Bb clarinet, and bassoon. It begins with a waltz tune in 3/4 time for flute and oboe in close thirds, while the English horn plays a rhythmic countermelody and the bassoon plays a rising and falling scale. The tune is picked up by the clarinet and bassoon, while the flute has the countermelody and the English horn has the scales. This is followed by a pair of themes for oboe and clarinet, one of which is a variant on the original theme. These themes are picked up by the English horn and bassoon. A theme which is a variant of the original theme is continued by the clarinet, while the flute plays the original theme, the bassoon has the countermelody, and the English horn has the scales. The new theme is continued by the oboe and the clarinet, while the bassoon has the original theme, with the flute taking it over while the oboe has the countermelody and the English horn and clarinet have the scales. This leads to a section in 6/8 time, with a pair of new countermelodies by the flute and oboe, then taken up by the oboe and bassoon, then by the flute and English horn, then by the oboe and clarinet, and finally by the flute and clarinet. This leads to a new section in 4/4 time, which introduces three new themes, for flute, oboe, and clarinet, and these are traded around among the instruments. The piece ends with a reprise of the opening section, in 3/4 time. The piece is comprised of 13 dreams, and is 3:50 minutes long.

Eight of Swords

In the Waite deck, there is a woman, bound and hoodwinked, with eight swords about her. Waite associates this card with "bad news, violent chagrin, crisis, censure, power in trammels, conflict, also sickness." Case has "indecision, waste of energy in details, a crisis." In the Pholarcos deck, a man in pain with curly hair and eyes partially shut has the image of a bird piercing an infinity symbol at his ajna center. Below are eight breath spirals, and the man holds an alembic containing a smaller version of himself, which is trying to break free. The words "negotiate your rebirth" appear on his blue robe. Sorrenti states, "and here your mind becomes your trap, not your flight. Undo the twist of rope around your neck, call in the nightingale's song." Common dream themes include male figures (5), female figures (3), food (3), trees (2), golf courses (2), and the colors black (2) and white (2). Common emotions include surprise (3) and interest/disinterest (3).

This piece is in D major, Allegretto, and is scored for woodwind quartet. It begins in 3/4 time with a rather bouncy four-bar theme for the oboe, later joined by the clarinet. The tune is broken into two-bar segments, and the pieces are traded among the four instruments, with a jaunty countermelody accompanying it. This countermelody continues while a new two-bar theme is introduced on the flute, followed by the oboe, and the bassoon, followed by a unison passage. This leads to a section in 4/4 time, with four new themes tossed around among the instruments. The piece concludes with a reprise of the opening theme on oboe and bassoon, on flute and clarinet, and last by all four instruments in unison. The piece is comprised of 9 dreams, and is 2:55 minutes long.

Nine of Swords

In the Waite deck, there is a woman seated on her couch in lamentation, with nine swords over her. Waite associates this card with "death, failure, miscarriage, delay, deception, disappointment, despair." Case has "worry, suffering, despair, misery, loss." In the Pholarcos deck, a man stands within an oval, and from his open mouth emerge nine breath spirals. The lower part of his body is a dagger. Three birds approach him on the right, while six approach from above left – perhaps in attack, perhaps not. Sorrenti states, "A nightmare sucks you into its turmoil yet watch carefully – nightmares are frogs ready to be kissed, creatures requiring your attention. Are those daggers or angels pointing at you?" Common dream themes include conferences (3), female figures (3), and roads (2).

This piece is in G minor, Allegro, and is in 4/4 time throughout. It is scored for flute, clarinet, bassoon, and hand cymbals. It is essentially a tango, whose main theme is first introduced by the flute, while the clarinet and cymbals play a rhythmic underlay and the bassoon plays ascending scales. This is not entirely out of keeping with Waite's interpretation, as the tango is historically associated with both seduction and knife fighting![1] This is followed by a restatement of the tango theme on the clarinet, while the flute has the rhythmic underlay. The bassoon then plays a countermelody, while the other instruments have syncopations. The main theme returns as before, followed by a second excursion on the clarinet. There is a grand pause, and the original tango theme picks up again as before, on the flute. The piece is comprised of 5 dreams, and is 3:15 minutes long.

Ten of Swords

In the Waite deck, there is a prostrate figure, pierced by ten swords. These penetrate the body, many at the chakra points. Waite associates this card with "pain, affliction, tears, sadness, desolation." Case has "ruin, pain, sudden misfortune . . . end of delusion." In the Pholarcos deck, the unblindfolded head of a woman faces front, while ten breath spirals accompanied by ten birds fly upwards. Ten sealed alembics are suspended from the top of the image, while an additional open alembic has released a phoenix with a red heart. The words "the grand experiment of life" are written below, and beside them is the Saturn-Sun-Moon spiral and a large dragonfly. Sorrenti states, "The awakening of Aquarian ideals. The experience is now electrified in all its details and story, eyes are open to the lucid dream of it, conscious of the fullness of this manifestation . . . In the grand experiment of life, can the mind be wide enough to invite all things?" There were no common dream themes. Warning/chiding (2) was a common emotion.

This piece is in D major, Allegro, and is in 4/4 time throughout. It is scored for flute, oboe, English horn, Bb clarinet, and bassoon. It begins with a simple tune for the oboe, which is picked up with slight overlap by the flute, with somewhat more overlap by the English horn, with yet more overlap by the clarinet, and with even more overlap by the bassoon – as if each instrument were intruding on its predecessor. The flute then plays a related countermelody, and is joined in close thirds in it by the oboe. This works its way down the set of instruments in pairs, and is followed by a restatement of the original theme on English horn, trodden upon by the oboe and then by the flute. This leads to a new and more rhythmic theme on flute and clarinet, followed by English horn and bassoon, followed by oboe and bassoon, followed by flute and clarinet. This is followed by a restatement of the original theme on the English horn, trodden upon by the clarinet, trodden upon by the bassoon. This leads to a restatement of the countermelody in descending pairs as before. The piece ends with a unison statement of the countermelody. The piece is comprised of 4 dreams, and is 3:30 minutes long.

---

[1] Marcelo Solis, The History of Tango. https://escuelatangoba.com/marcelosolis/category/history-of-tango/.

King of Swords

In the Waite deck, a king sits in judgment, holding an unsheathed sword. Waite associates this card with "judgment . . . power, command, authority, militant intelligence, law, offices of the crown." Case has "distrustful, suspicious man, full of ideas, thoughts, and designs . . . Care, observation, extreme caution." In the Pholarcos deck, the King is a thoughtful, fair-skinned man with one blue eye and one yellow eye. His crown is adorned with two birds. Sorrenti states, "The activity of the king's mind is visible through his skin. Speedy hummingbirds make his crown weightless. He conceptualizes clean as a knife, abstracts a sentence to lyrical flight, turns a phrase like clockwork, infuses you with ethical perspectives of generations past and future offspring measuring ideals, promethean enlightenments, ever expanding, vibrating, a vast growing arc of concept and contradiction, new realities downloading, sublimating, concretizing – everything is true and its opposite too." Male authority figures (2) are the only common dream themes. Emotional themes include opposition (2) and overcoming (2).

This piece is in D major, Allegro non Troppo, and is scored for flute, Bb clarinet, bassoon, snare drum, and bass drum. As do many of the pieces for the kings and queens, it begins with a fanfare, in 3/4 time for the bassoon, joined by the clarinet. The flute and snare drum begin a lively tune with dotted eighth and sixteenth notes, which is picked up by the clarinet and bassoon. This leads to a section in 4/4 time, in which the flute and clarinet play a call and response theme while the bassoon and snare drum play rhythmic eighth notes. These rhythmic eighth notes, now in arpeggios, are taken up by the flute while the clarinet plays a new theme and the bassoon continues the call-and-response theme. The flute and clarinet trade places while the bassoon continues. There is a reprise of the call-and-response theme on the flute and clarinet, and this leads to a restatement of the lively tune, again in 3/4 time, on the bassoon, followed by the clarinet, then by all three woodwind instruments. The piece is comprised of 3 dreams, and is 2:25 minutes long.

Queen of Swords

In the Waite deck, an enthroned queen holds a sword, vertically, in her right hand. Her left hand is extended, the arm raised, and her countenance is severe, chastened, and suggests familiarity with sorrow. Waite associates this card with "widowhood, female sadness and embarrassment, absence, sterility, mourning." Case has "widowhood, mourning, a keen, quick, intensely perceptive, subtle woman, usually fond of dancing." In the Pholarcos deck, the Queen is a mature woman in blue, standing at the highest observation point, carrying an owl on her left wrist while another perches on her left shoulder. Sorrenti states, "the path is full of scattered poems brought in by wind storms. You may feel like your skin is being read aloud and every one of your thoughts caught on the current." Common dream themes include female figures (9), vehicles (3), male figures (3), and animals (3). Common emotions include affection (3), concern (2), and relief (2).

This piece is in D major, Moderato. It is scored for woodwind quartet. It begins in 6/8 time with a lilting melody on the flute. This is picked up by the oboe, while the bassoon plays an inverted version of it, in contrary motion. The flute and clarinet play a similar duet, followed again by the oboe and bassoon. This leads to a section in 4/4 time, in which the flute, oboe, and clarinet each play a different theme. The bassoon joins them with one of the themes, a descending scale. This leads into a trio on two new themes on flute, oboe, and bassoon. This is followed by a restatement of the lilting theme in 6/8 time, first on oboe and bassoon, then on flute and clarinet, both with contrary motion, and finally on all four instruments. The piece is comprised of 10 dreams, and is 3:20 minutes long.

Knight of Swords

In the Waite deck, a horseman is in full course, as if scattering his enemies. Waite associates this card with "skill, bravery, capacity, defense, address, enmity, wrath, war, destruction, resistance, ruin." Case has "active, clever, subtle, skillful, domineering young man. Enmity, wrath, war." In the Pholarcos deck, the head of the goddess Sophia is shown, asleep, her head resting upon the upper part of a metal bird. Sorrenti states, "Just step though that small portal and meet the psychopomps who will ferry your journeys back and forth between the worlds . . . In the air, you will be led to calm the frenzied mind or to brilliant argument or the question: who is being dreamed?" Common dream themes include male figures (7), female figures (4), political parties (2), and music (2). Common emotional themes include decision (3), opposition/difficulty/limitation (3), and concern (2).

This piece is in Bb major, Moderato. It is scored for flute, clarinet, bassoon, and snare drum. It begins in 4/4 time with a tattoo on the drum, which is maintained throughout the piece. The bassoon, at least at first, mimics the rhythm of the drum, while the flute states a martial, declarative melody. This is then taken up by the clarinet, and then by the bassoon, while the clarinet has the rhythmic figure. The clarinet plays a variation on this tune, with accompaniments from the other two wind instruments. This is then taken up by the flute and then by the bassoon. The clarinet continues this theme while the other instruments play countermelodies. This leads to a section in 3/4 time which is an adaptation of the original theme, first on the flute, then on the flute and clarinet together, while the bassoon plays a countermelody. The piece is comprised of 13 dreams, and is 3:25 minutes long.

Page of Swords

In the Waite deck, a lithe, active figure holds a sword upright in both hands, while in the act of swift walking. Waite associates this card with "authority, overseeing, secret service, vigilance, spying, examination." Case has "vigilant, acute, subtle, active youth." In the Pholarcos deck, a young woman rides on the back of a raven. The skull of a bull is above. Sorrenti states, "She's often busy championing the underdog babies and she offers classes on the theory of knowledge – and she may lend you thaumaturgical words for a rough night," Common dream themes include male figures (4), female figures (3), evil (2), groups of people (2), friends (2), dwellings (2), food (2), and computer programs (2). Hope (2) was a common emotion.

This piece is in Bb major, Andante. It is scored for woodwind quartet. It opens in 3/4 time with a pair of simple tunes played on flute and bassoon. This is followed by a section in 6/8 time, with an opening tune on the flute, followed by the oboe and clarinet together in close thirds, and then by the bassoon. This leads to a section in 4/4 time, in which the flute and oboe play countermelodies, with an ostinato below on clarinet and bassoon. The ostinato continues in the flute, while the other 3 instruments play countermelodies. The clarinet plays an aria-like theme, while the other instruments play countermelodies around it. This is then picked up by the flute, with the other instruments playing the countermelodies. These continue as the flute introduces a new theme. This leads to a reprise of the opening, with the themes played on flute and clarinet. The piece is comprised of 12 dreams, and is 4:40 minutes long.

♦ 12 ♦
The Minor Arcana – Pentacles

A total of 139 dreams were associated with Pentacles: 113 with dream text, 24 without dream text, and 3 duplicates. Although Db/C# major could have been used for these compositions, only the Earth element keys F major and A major and their relative minors were used. Altogether, the fourteen Pentacles pieces are 47:20 minutes in length.

Ace of Pentacles

In the Waite deck, a hand, issuing from a cloud, holds a pentacle. Waite associates this card with "perfect contentment, felicity, ecstasy – also speedy intelligence, gold." Case has "material gain, wealth, contentment." In the Pholarcos deck, there is a hoodwinked female figure with jasmine flowers and marigold and sage leaves emerging from her head. Sorrenti states, "that which makes rock and bone and gold . . . The joy of flesh, the workings of nature and the visible world, wealth." Common dream themes include archaeological sites (2) and artifacts (2).

This piece is in F major, and is in 4/4 time throughout, Vivace. It is scored for glockenspiel, vibraphone, chimes, and marimba. It opens with a set of ascending and descending scales on the marimba, which is a motif which is carried throughout the piece by one or another of the instruments. Above this, a dance-like tune is played in close thirds by the glockenspiel and vibraphone, then joined by the chimes. After the first statement of the tune, the glockenspiel and vibraphone play a countermelody, still in close thirds. The dance tune, also, is played throughout the piece, distributed among the four instruments, sometimes with variations, sometimes in harmony, sometimes in canon, and sometimes above countermelodies. The piece closes with a reprise of the original dance tune followed by its countermelody. The piece is comprised of 4 dreams, and is 2:20 minutes long.

Two of Pentacles

In the Waite deck, a young man in the act of dancing has a pentacle in either hand, and they are joined by a cord in the shape of an infinity sign. Waite associates this card with "gaiety, recreation and its connections . . . news and messages in writing, such as obstacles, agitation, trouble, embroilment." Case has "harmony in midst of change." In the Pholarcos deck, a sphere separates into a pair of jagged leaves extending, one from above, one from below, while a bull scatters flowers. The Saturn-Sun-Moon spiral is present, and the words "for the joy of it" are adjacent to the bull's head. Sorrenti states, "It is as the trees of the great religions where the roots are in heaven and the foliage spreads on earth. Creativity invites beauty forth to express what shapes we've taken. Juggle color, stripe and coin, they will keep coming." Common dream themes include textiles (2), groups of people (2), and the colors red (2) and green (2).

This piece is in A major, Vivace, and is in 4/4 time throughout. It is scored for vibraphone, guitar, and harp. It opens with a steady quarter-note phrase in the vibraphone and left hand of the harp. This steady beat continues throughout most of the piece on one or another of the instruments. The guitar enters above this with a theme, while the harp plays arpeggios – these arpeggios also continue throughout the rest of the piece on one or another of the instruments. The harp introduces a new melody, which is picked up by the guitar and then by the vibraphone. This is followed by two new themes on the harp against arpeggios on the vibraphone and the steady phrase in the guitar. The vibraphone introduces a new theme, which is picked up by the harp. This leads to a reprise of the original guitar theme against the steady phrase on vibraphone and the harp, along with arpeggios. The piece is comprised of 8 dreams, and is 2:35 minutes long.

Three of Pentacles

In the Waite deck, there is a sculptor at work in a monastery. Waite associates this card with "metier, trade, skilled labor . . . nobility, aristocracy, renown, glory." Case has "construction, material increase, growth, financial gain." In the Pholarcos deck, a woman with three circles tattooed on her right arm is in the lower right. To the left, standing upon a base of vines, a man drops three balls with spirals in them. In the upper right is a sitar player. Sorrenti states, "The green energy surges up through the roots, grounding their endeavor. Chords strum a smooth preparation, performers gather to rehearse . . . A Persian tale smelling of ambrosia and myrrh." Common dream themes include bakery items (2) and male figures (2). Complaint/reprimand (2) was a common emotion.

This piece is in A major, and is in 4/4 time throughout, Allegro. It is scored for vibraphone, guitar, and marimba. It opens with a melody on guitar, which is picked up by the vibraphone while the marimba plays arpeggios. The vibraphone and guitar play countermelodies while the marimba has descending scales. The piece concludes with a reprise of the original theme on vibraphone and guitar, while the marimba plays arpeggios. The piece is comprised of 3 dreams, and is 2:20 minutes long.

Four of Pentacles

In the Waite deck, a crowned figure, having a pentacle over his crown, clasps another pentacle with his hands and arms; two more pentacles are under his feet. Waite associates this card with "the surety of possessions, cleaving to that which one has, gifts, legacy, inheritance." Case has "earthly power, physical forces, skill in directing them." In the Pholarcos deck, the god Apollo pounces from above, right, and emits a ray of energy from his mouth which strikes Cassandra, who is bound in a net, in the heart, negating her gift of prophecy. Below her are four pumpkins, and the words "Apollo's curse." Sorrenti states, "Your palm stays empty and begins to itch, your throat shrinks . . . receive past the hauntings of empty rooms where spiders scurry and bluebirds sing for no one." Common dream themes include music (5), female figures (5), male figures (3), leather (2), Germans (2), rooms (2), notebooks (2), and lunch (2). Surprise (2) was a common emotion.

This piece is in F major, and is in 4/4 time throughout, Allegro. It is scored for vibraphone, guitar, and marimba. It opens with a rapid ascending series of syncopated sixteenth and eighth notes on the marimba, similar to a Latin rumba rhythm. This is picked up on the guitar, while the marimba plays arpeggios over it. Either the rumba rhythm or the arpeggios, or both, continue throughout the entire piece, on one instrument or another. The vibraphone and the marimba play an obbligato in close thirds over this. Then they play a pair of countermelodies, which are picked up by the marimba and the guitar. The marimba plays another pair of countermelodies while the vibraphone has the rumba rhythm. Another pair of countermelodies is presented by the vibraphone and the guitar, while the marimba has the rumba. Then two new countermelodies are introduced on the vibraphone and marimba, while the guitar has arpeggios. The piece ends with a reprise of the obbligato melody in the vibraphone and marimba. It is comprised of 13 dreams, and is 3:45 minutes long.

Five of Pentacles

In the Waite deck, two mendicants in a snowstorm pass a lighted casement, in whose stained glass window five pentacles appear. Waite associates this card with "material trouble above all . . . destitution . . . love and lovers . . . also concordance, affinities." Case has "concordance, affinity, adaptation." In the Pholarcos deck, a pensive female figure stands, her right fist clenched, and five balls with spirals pass at the level of her head. A fox and a wolf emanate from the bed sheet which binds her body, and the wolf is howling, accompanied by the words "howls of healing". Sorrenti states, "A figure at war with reality, either because circumstances are too harsh or because her ability to cope is fragile. Know there are always inner lairs where the wild ones can rekindle faith – you may have to seek them outside." There were no common dream themes. Wonder/admiration (2) was a common emotion.

This piece is in A major, Allegretto. I had originally scored it for harp solo, but my wife's harp teacher commented that it did not sound sufficiently "harpistic", so I rescored it for two guitars. It opens with a syncopated rhythm in 4/4 time, which develops into a melody in the first guitar. This is followed by a variation on the same melody, while the second guitar continues to play syncopations. This leads to a middle section in 3/4 time, in which a new melody is introduced on the first guitar while the second guitar plays arpeggios; then they switch places. The piece ends with a restatement of the opening music in 4/4 time. The piece is comprised of 4 dreams, and is 1:35 minutes long, the shortest of all of the Minor Arcana pieces.

Six of Pentacles

In the Waite deck, a merchant weighs money in a pair of scales and distributes it to the needy and distressed. Waite associates this card with "presents, gifts, gratification . . . attention, vigilance, now is the accepted time, present prosperity." Case has "material prosperity, philanthropy, presents." In the Pholarcos deck, a short-haired young blonde woman stands in a rose garden, with six red roses to the left. There are six balls in an "X" pattern below. Above is the Saturn-Sun-Moon spiral, and an angelic figure with the written words, "hear the plants' poetics." Sorrenti states, "There is always enough for all, and always enough space in the heart to hold all things – gifts come to light, great generosity." Common dream themes include groups (4), training (2), printed material (2), and conflict (2). Charity (2) was a common emotion.

This piece is in A major, in 3/4 time throughout, Andantino. It is scored for harp, with a simple triangle accompaniment on the downbeat of each measure. It opens with a simple tune accompanied by arpeggios. After a brief transition, there is a waltz tune, also accompanied by arpeggios. Three further waltz tunes follow, and the piece ends with a reprise of the opening tune. The piece is comprised of 6 dreams, and is 3:50 minutes long.

Seven of Pentacles

In the Waite deck, a young man, leaning on his staff, looks intently at seven pentacles attached to a clump of greenery on his right. Waite associates this card with "money, business, barter. . . altercation, quarrel . . . innocence, ingenuity, purgation." Case has "success unfulfilled, delay, but growth." In the Pholarcos deck, a red-haired female artist with paw prints on her cheeks holds a green toad in her left hand, and her wrist grows roots. She is merged with the spirit of a tree. A series of seven balls with spirals is tattooed on her forearm. Sorrenti states, "Take time to listen. Take stock. Make friends with toad camouflaged on mossy stone; he will flatten his belly as he shares secrets with you about water and earthquakes and the night." Common dream themes include male figures (6), female figures (5), groups (3), numbers (3), Tennessee (2), music (2), food (2), books (2), and enemies (2).

This piece is in F major, Vivace, and is scored for marimba — one of only two solo pieces in the entire set. However, as noted in Chapter Five,[1] it requires two performers, so it is not really a solo. It opens in 4/4 time with a simple melody, followed by a countermelody, followed by a restatement of the original melody. This is followed by a variation on the same melody. This transitions to a section in 3/4 time, on a similar melody and countermelody. A new melody is introduced, followed by another. This leads to a reprise of the original melody, again in 4/4 time. The piece ends with a rapid coda. It is comprised of 16 dreams, and is 5:15 minutes long.

Eight of Pentacles

In the Waite deck, an artist in stone is at work. Waite associates this card with "work, employment, commission, craftsmanship, skill in craft and business." Case has "skill in material affairs." In the Pholarcos deck, a thoughtful man is learning to use a diamond polishing mill. Two joined hexagrams in hexagons, representing sacred union, are to his right, and eight balls with spirals are above. The words "Apprenticing infinity in the here and now . . . the love that I feel for you is always love for you" are written below. Sorrenti states, "Make the diamond body." Common dream themes include female figures (2), music (2), food (2), and male figures (2).

This piece is in A major, Moderato, and is scored for xylophone, marimba, and piano. It opens in 4/4 time with a theme on xylophone and accompaniment on marimba, which is then picked up by the piano. This is followed by a section in which three themes are played against one another on the three instruments. This is followed by a waltz tune in 3/4 time for piano, which is picked up on the marimba with xylophone accompaniment. The piano responds with a countermelody, which is picked up by the other two instruments. A section in 4/4 time follows, with new themes shared by the three instruments. The piece ends with a reprise of the original theme and accompaniment, on all three instruments. The piece is comprised of 9 dreams, and is 3:45 minutes long.

Nine of Pentacles

In the Waite deck, a woman with a bird on her wrist stands amidst a great abundance of grapevines in the garden of a great house. Waite associates this card with "prudence, safety, success, accomplishment, certitude, discernment." Case has "prudence, material gain, completion." In the Pholarcos deck, a jolly bearded man seated on a pedestal of vines holds six spiral balls in his hands, while three more are in his lap. He is surrounded by an oval which has nine more spiral balls placed at intervals, in a background of green leaves. Sorrenti states, "He is secure in his accomplishments, a peaceful oak with strong roots. The riches of your life glow on your lap; hard

---

[1] See supra, p. 33

won or pure gift, the bounty of life caresses you and all is in its place." Common dream themes include female figures (4), male figures (4), groups (4), music (3), open areas (3), children (2), boxes (2), and foreign countries (2). Surprise (2) was a common emotion.

This piece is in F major, in 4/4 time, Allegro Molto. It is scored for glockenspiel, xylophone, chimes, harp, snare drum, and bass drum. It opens with a march for all five instruments. This is followed by a somewhat jazzy tune on piano, with xylophone accompaniment, which is punctuated at the end by a sforzando xylophone glissando. The chimes and harp introduce a variation on the jazz tune, with an underlay of syncopated notes on the piano and persistent quarter notes on the xylophone and chimes. This is followed by a rapid tune on the harp, while the glockenspiel has the syncopations and the chimes have a countermelody. This is followed by a lyrical melody on the harp, with arpeggios on piano. This is followed by a reprise of the jazz variation on chimes and harp, with countermelodies as before. The piece concludes with a reprise of the opening march, punctuated by the xylophone glissando. The piece is comprised of 17 dreams, and is 3:45 minutes long.

Ten of Pentacles

In the Waite deck, a man and a woman stand beneath an archway which gives entrance to a house and domain. A set of ten pentacles in the configuration of the Tree of Life is under the arch. Waite associates this card with "gain, riches, family matters, archives, extraction, the abode of a family." Case has "wealth, riches, material prosperity." In the Pholarcos deck, an unblindfolded woman with green eyes has a four-pointed star at her brow; a white jasmine flower is in her hair, and a dragonfly is above. A stream of open-eyed sage leaves flutters down on one side. She wears a necklace of ten spiral balls. The Saturn-Sun-Moon spiral is below. Sorrenti states, "Legacy and continuity, so much has been built, such lavish gardens for the children to play in." Common dream themes include male figures (4), female figures (3), children (3), groups (3), houses (2), murder mysteries (2), books (2), and the color blue (2). Surprise/amazement (3) was a common emotion.

This piece is in F major, Andante, and is scored for harp solo – the only truly solo piece in the set. It begins with a gentle waltz tune, with arpeggios, in 3/4 time. This is followed by a countermelody, and it leads to a section in 6/8 time which introduces a new theme. There is a brief transition section in 3/4 time, which leads to a section in 4/4 time with a new melody and underlying countermelody. Another new melody with countermelody is introduced. This leads to a reprise of the opening waltz in 3/4 time, with the melody played an octave higher. The piece is comprised of 10 dreams, and is 6:25 minutes long.

King of Pentacles

In the Waite deck, there is an enthroned king, with a rather dark visage, suggesting courage, but somewhat lethargic in tendency. Waite associates this card with "valor, realizing intelligence, business and normal intellectual aptitude, sometimes mathematical gifts and entertainments of this kind." Case has "friendly, steady, reliable married man." In the Pholarcos deck, the King is in the guise of the antlered Celtic god Cernunnos, with the symbols of the alchemical elements on his headband. Sorrenti states, "A midnight sun streams through the king. From an unfathomable distance the dream brings back the rich spirals of his manifestation . . . until the creature is alive and standing before him." Common dream themes include male authority figures (8), employment (2), female figures (2), food (2), water (2), children (2), trickery (2), collapse/overthrow (2), and the color black (2). Common emotions include victory (2), success (2), and tyranny (2).

This piece is in F major, in 4/4 time throughout, Allegro Molto. It is scored for glockenspiel, vibraphone, piano, and timpani. It opens with a fanfare on vibraphone, piano, and timpani. This is followed by a tune on glockenspiel, accompanied by a countermelody on the piano and arpeggios on the vibraphone. The piano then takes up the melody, with the countermelody on the glockenspiel. A fragment of the countermelody forms the basis of a new, rhythmic tune on the glockenspiel, which is taken up by the vibraphone and piano. A new melody is introduced on the piano which is taken up in canon by the vibraphone. The opening fanfare is played against this on the glockenspiel, and then on the vibraphone. The rhythmic tune is then repeated on the glockenspiel, which then introduces a new rhythmic figure against syncopations on the piano. The piece ends with a reprise of the opening fanfare, at first on glockenspiel and vibraphone with a piano countermelody, then these roles are reversed, and finally the fanfare is played by all four instruments, with a brief 1-5-1 coda. The piece is comprised of 15 dreams, and is 3:50 minutes long.

Queen of Pentacles

In the Waite deck, there is an enthroned queen, whose face suggests a dark woman whose qualities might be summed up in the idea of greatness of soul. She contemplates a pentacle and she may see many worlds there. Waite associates this card with "opulence, magnificence, generosity, security, liberty." Case has "generous, intelligent, charming, moody married woman." In the Pholarcos deck, the Queen is a mature woman with one breast bared, riding on a bull. Eight spiral balls fashioned from Etruscan gold emanate from her head. Sorrenti states, "Waking into the color of morning Glory, there is such pleasure to be had in this dawn . . . They are used to the Queen . . . Any touch from her fills them with the flavor of self-worth." Common dream themes include music (4), male figures (3), female figures (3), groups (3), Christian religious figures (2), and foreign countries (2). Concern (2), challenge (2), and skepticism/disbelief (2) were common emotions.

This piece is in F major, in 3/4 time throughout, Allegro. It is scored for glockenspiel, guitar, and piano. It opens with a simple waltz tune on the glockenspiel, with arpeggios on the guitar. The piano plays another simple waltz tune, with continued arpeggios from the guitar. The glockenspiel plays another simple waltz tune, with countermelody and arpeggios in the piano. The glockenspiel and guitar play contrasting phrases, which are repeated by the piano. The piano then plays yet another simple waltz, followed by a pair of countermelodies on guitar and piano, while the glockenspiel has arpeggios. The piece ends with a reprise of the original waltz tune on piano, with continued arpeggios on the glockenspiel. The piece is comprised of 14 dreams, and is 3:25 minutes long.

Knight of Pentacles

In the Waite deck, there is a horseman on a slow, enduring, heavy horse. Waite associates this card with "utility, interest, servicableness, rectitude, responsibility." Case has "laborious, patient, dull young man." In the Pholarcos deck, there is the figure of a kindly, bearded man holding a spiral ball, with artemisia growing from his head. A dragonfly is to the right, and the words "written in blood & earth" are below. Sorrenti states, "He creates rituals for worship and clay bowls that hold water for the ancestor. His throat chakra is glowing, aligning personal song. In earth, you will be led to perseverance, sensuality, the magic of matter, protecting what you hold dear." Common dream themes include male figures (7), groups (4), food (3), music (3), conflict (3), female figures (3), animals (3), hills (2), and vehicles (2). Common emotions included success (3), sadness (2), and hope (2).

This piece is in F major, and is in 3/4 time throughout, Allegro Vivace. It is scored for glockenspiel, vibraphone, marimba, and timpani. The timpani sets up a rocking rhythm, over which the vibraphone plays a lively, bouncing rhythm reminiscent of a horse galloping. This is picked up by the marimba and then by the glockenspiel. The marimba then introduces a new theme, which has a countermelody on the glockenspiel. This is followed by a simple waltz tune on the glockenspiel with countermelodies on the marimba and then on the vibraphone. This is followed by another 2-bar galloping theme which is tossed back and forth among the instruments. The waltz tune returns, on marimba, with a countermelody on the glockenspiel. Another new theme is introduced on the glockenspiel and vibraphone, while the marimba has a countermelody. At the end, the glockenspiel and vibraphone introduce another waltz tune, with a countermelody on the marimba. The piece is comprised of 15 dreams, and is 2:35 minutes long.

Page of Pentacles

In the Waite deck, a youthful figure looks intently at the pentacle that hovers over his raised hands. Waite associates this card with "application, study scholarship, reflection . . . news, messages and the bringer thereof – also rule, management." Case has "diligent, careful, deliberate youth." In the Pholarcos deck, there is a red-haired woman, asleep, with a sunny garden growing from her head. Sorrenti states, "Correspondences true throughout creation. Geography and spatial relations become a language that carries meaning . . . keep learning." Male figures (2) were the only common dream themes.

This piece is in A major, Allegro Vivace. It is scored for vibraphone, guitar, and marimba. It opens with a syncopated figure in 4/4 time on the guitar, followed by some rapid ascending and descending scales. The marimba adds an ornamented version of the same figure. The vibraphone plays a new theme, underlain by syncopation on the marimba. The opening section is reprised on guitar and marimba. This is followed by a section in 6/8 time, with a tune on vibraphone and a triplet underlay on the guitar. At the end, the opening section is reprised on guitar and marimba, with the vibraphone joining in. The piece is comprised of 4 dreams, and is 2:00 minutes long.

◆ 13 ◆
How to Access and Use the Music Files

As I indicated in Chapter Two, my main objective in agreeing to undertake this project was service: that is, the music which I received in my dreams over the course of 19 months is intended to be used, otherwise the project will merely have been an exercise in self-indulgence. I envision that it could be used by anyone who uses the Tarot, whether for their own spiritual development, or as a guide for others who come to them for advice, or even potentially in healing.

As a further confirmation of this, I took an I Ching reading after the conclusion of the project, and the result was Hexagram 30, Li, which consists of repeated trigrams of Li, The Clinging, Fire, with no change lines. The Wilhelm/Baynes translation[1], which is the one I find most reliable, gives the associated image for this Hexagram:

> That which is bright rises twice;
>
> The image of Fire.
>
> Thus the great man, by perpetuating this brightness,
>
> Illumines the four quarters of the world.

Wilhelm further comments,

> *Each of the two trigrams represents the sun in the course of a day. The two together represent the repeated movement of the sun, the function of light with respect to time. The great man continues the work of nature in the human world. Through the clarity of his nature he causes the light to spread farther and farther and to penetrate the nature of man ever more deeply.*

This seems to me to be a perfectly clear validation of my intention for this project.

Now that the entire set is completed, I have made it available as a website which users of the Tarot can access, so that they can click on an audio link accompanied by an icon drawn from Carmen Sorrenti's Pholarcos Deck for each card they have drawn and hear the music for it[2]. A suggestion

---

[1] Helmut Wilhelm, *The I Ching, or Book of Changes*. Trans. Cary F. Baynes. Bollingen Series XIX. Princeton University Press, Princeton NJ, 1967, p.119. I would note that I began to rely upon the I Ching for decision-making several years before I was exposed to the Tarot.

[2] I have chosen the Pholarcos deck for the website icons, for the principal reason that Sorrenti's Minor Arcana are both more symbolically nuanced and more artistically rendered than those in the Rider/Waite deck; the Case deck uses only geometric forms for the numbered Minor Keys.

about the structure of this website was provided to me in a referential dream:

> *I see the structure of the website which will be used for access to the Musical Dream Tarot. For each of the Minor Arcana, there is a circular elemental colored icon (I see green for Pentacles) to the left of the number of the Key which the user can click on to get a performance of the music for that Key. For the Major Arcana, the icons are small images of the keys, followed by their number and name. Similarly, the user would click on the icon to get the performance of the music.*

This dream was a major advance in the design of the final product of the Musical Dream Tarot project, but some modifications of the details were needed to make this practically workable. The card images appear above the audio links, which are rectangular rather than circular in shape.

To create the final files for the website, I first converted the raw Finale© (.musx) files to .wav files – Finale© has a utility for that – and then I used Switch Sound File Converter©[3] to convert the .wav files to .mp3 format. Then I used a website creator, Squarespace©[4], to set up the structure of the website, with initial assistance from my Anthropology Department colleague, Dr. Michael Zimmerman, and from Matt DeGrechie at Bridgewater State's IT Support facility.

The website is accessible at www.musicaldreamtarot.com. It is organized into five sections, one for the Major Arcana and one for each of the four Minor Arcana suits, each headed with the "Shapeshifter" image. The icons and links to the music files in each section are displayed below the section title on each page. Each entry has a thumbnail image of the Key from the Pholarcos deck framed within its elemental or zodiacal color (as suggested in the dream above), and below

---

In addition, very similar to the Musical Dream Tarot, its images are based upon a long series of her own dreams. As noted in Chapter Four, Sorrenti has introduced a number of innovations in her deck: specifically, the suits which appear on the Keys on the website are Sparks (= Wands), Coral (= Cups), Wings (= Swords), and Spirals (= Pentacles). In addition, the Knights and Pages of the traditional deck have been replaced by Trails and Dreamers, respectively. Finally, following one line of traditional placements, she has reversed the positions of the Major Arcana Keys Strength (= Key 8 in Waite and Case; Key 11 in Pholarcos) and Justice (= Key 11 in Waite and Case; Key 8 in Pholarcos). In the names assigned to the Minor Suits and Keys on the website, I have retained the traditional nomenclature, and I have also retained the Waite/Case positions of Keys 8 and 11, for the reason that the images on them correspond so clearly to the astrological signs of Leo and Libra, respectively, and they are therefore shown in their order among the astrological signs.

[3] Switch-Sound File Converter, https://www.nch.com.au/switch/index.html?ns=true&kw=switch%20sound% 20file%20converter&gclid=EAlaIQobChMI6_SFucDC_QIVB__jBx0j5gBgEAAYASAAE gL8GfD_BwE

[4] Squarespace, https://www.squarespace.com/.

the Key is an audio link to the .mp3 music file, with the title of the Key. Click once on the audio link arrow and the music will come up. The Keys and the audio links may be accessed either in landscape format, as on a laptop computer, or in portrait format, as on a mobile phone.

What I suggest is that while listening to each musical piece, you meditate upon the imagery of the Key. This will be most likely to stimulate intuitive responses, as you allow your consciousness to drift along with the music while concentrating upon the image. If the Key is being used for healing purposes, for yourself or for others, you could concentrate upon the part of the body in need of healing, using the correspondences provided in Chapter Eight for the Major Arcana. I also recommend that those who are interested in this form of service should study the healing techniques described by the Tibetan in his volume, *Esoteric Healing*.[5]

I have enlisted students in the Bridgewater State University Wind Band to produce live performances of some of the pieces in the set. Funding for student stipends has been provided by a generous grant from the Bridgewater State University Retired Faculty Club. As these live performances are recorded, I intend to replace the computer-generated .mp3 files with them, over time. I look forward to being able to share the results of this project with a wider audience! For questions, and requests for scores and parts for performances, I can be contacted at m.d.tarot@comcast.net.

---

[5] Alice A. Bailey, *Esoteric Healing*. Lucis Publishing, New York, 1980.

Bibliography

Aserinsky, Eugene, and Nathaniel Kleitman

    1993 Regularly Occurring Periods of Eye Motility, and Concomitant Phenomena during Sleep. *Science.* 1953:118:273–4.

Bach, Johann Sebastian

    n.d. *The Saint Matthew Passion.* https://www.youtube.com/watch?v=Tq4lxMcwYwU.

Bailey, Alice A.

    1922 *Letters on Occult Meditation.* Lucis Publishing, New York.

    1922 *The Consciousness of the Atom.* Lucis Publishing, New York.

    1925 *A Treatise on Cosmic Fire.* Lucis Publishing, New York.

    1927 *The Light of the Soul: The Yoga Sutras of Patanjali.* Lucis Publishing, New York.

    1932 *From Intellect to Intuition.* Lucis Publishing, New York.

    1934 *A Treatise on White Magic.* Lucis Publishing, New York.

    1936 *Esoteric Psychology*, v. 1. Lucis Publishing, New York.

    1951a *Esoteric Astrology.* Lucis Publishing, New York.

    1951b *The Unfinished Autobiography.* Lucis Publishing, New York.

    1960 *The Rays and the Initiations.* Lucis Publishing, New York.

    1980 *Esoteric Healing.* Lucis Publishing, New York.

Campbell, Joseph

    Pre-1970 Audio Lectures, Series One. https://jcf.org/lectures/.

Caroso, Fabritio

    n.d. Laura Suave. From *The Nobility of Ladies.* https://sonichits.com/video/Fabritio_Caroso/Laura_Suave? track=1.

Case, Paul Foster

    1947 *The Tarot: A Key to the Wisdom of the Ages.* Macoy Publishing Company, Richmond VA.

des Pres, Josquin

    n.d. Vive le Roi. https://www.youtube.com/watch?v=Z3rpUscM9KQ.

Freemasonry Network

    n.d. https://freemasonry.network/freemasonry-and-god/great-architect-universe/.

Freud, Sigmund

    2000 *The Interpretation of Dreams*. Oxford University Press, Oxford UK.

Handel, Georg Frederic

    n.d. *Judas Maccabeus*. https://www.youtube.com/watch?v=8p1BedwyFKY.

Hardin, Craig, ed.

    1951 *The Complete Works of Shakespeare*. Scott, Foresman, and Co., Chicago IL.

Hobb, Robin (Megan Lindholm)

    1997 *Assassin's Quest*. Bantam Books, New York.

Hoffman, Curtiss

    1974 *The Lion, the Eagle, the Man, and the Bull in Mesopotamian Glyptic*. University Microfilms, Ann Arbor MI.

    2003 South Brook Archaeological Survey. On file at the Massachusetts Historical Commission, Boston MA.

    2021 Dreaming in the Digging Fields. *International Journal of Dream Research* 14(2), 2021. *https://journals.ub.uni-heidelberg.de/index.php/IJoDR/article/view/76699.*

Jaspers, Karl

    2011 *The Origin and Goal of History*. Routledge Revivals, Milton Park, UK, 2011.

Jung, Carl Gustav

    1957-1977 *Collected Works*. 20 volumes. *Bollingen Series* XX. Trans. R.F.C. Hull. Princeton University Press, Princeton NJ.

    2009 *The Red Book*: *Liber Novus*. Ed. and trans. Sonu Shamdasani. W.W.Norton & Company, New York.

Jung, Carl Gustav, and Wolfgang Pauli

    1970 Synchronicity: An Acausal Connecting Principle. In *The Structure and Dynamics of the Psyche*. *Collected Works* v.8, *Bollingen Series* XX. Trans R.F.C. Hull. Princeton University Press, Princeton NJ.

Kaplan, Aryeh, trans.

    1997 *Sefer Yetzirah: The Book of Creation*. Weiser Books, New York.

Kaplan-Williams, Strephon

    1991 *Dream Cards: Understand Your Dreams and Enrich Your Life*. Fireside, Gleneden Beach, OR.

Kepler, Johannes

    1997 *The Harmony of the World*. Translated by Aiton, E. J.; Duncan, A. M. Field, J. American Philosophical Society, Philadelphia, PA.

King, Charles

    n.d. The Gnostics and Their Remains. http://www.luxlapis.co.za/at/serapis.htm.

Lennon, John, and Paul McCartney

    n.d. All You Need is Love. https://www.youtube.com/watch?v=_7xMfIp-irg.

Levi, Eliphas (Alphonse Louis Constant)

    2013 *The Key to the Mysteries*. Martino Fine Books, Eastford CT.

Levi-Strauss, Claude

    1966 *The Savage Mind*. University of Chicago Press, Chicago IL.

    1969 *The Raw and the Cooked*. Trans. John and Doreen Weightman. Harper and Row, New York.

Magnum, John

    n.d. https://www.laphil.com/musicdb/pieces/4455/variations-for-cello-and-piano-on-see-the-conquering-hero-comes-from-handels-judas-maccabaeus.

Matt, Daniel C., trans.

    2003 *The Zohar*. Stanford University Press, Palo Alto CA.

Modern Philosophy Standards

    n.d. https://modernphilosophystandards.com/2-the-universe/the-kabbalah-ain-soph-aur-and-heavenly-father/.

Nielsen, Tore

    2012 Variations in Dream Recall Frequency and Dream Theme Diversity by Age and Sex. *Frontiers in Neurology,* July.

Ouspensky, P.D.

    1931 *A New Model of the Universe*. Borzoi Books, New York.

Payne-Towler, Christine

    n.d. The Esoteric Origins of Tarot. https://www.tarot.com/tarot/christine-payne-towler/esoteric-origins.

Richman-Abdou, Kelly

    n.d. The Spellbinding History of Tarot Cards, from a Mainstream Card Game to a Magical Ritual. https://mymodernmet.com/history-of-tarot-cards/.

Schneider, Lauren

    2021 *Tarotpy©: It's All in the Cards*. New Insights Press, Los Angeles CA.

Schwartz, Stephen

    n.d. Prepare Ye the Way of the Lord. *Godspell*. https://www.youtube.com/watch?v=c1SiaCV26aQ.

Shainberg, Catherine

    2022 *The Kabbalah of Light*. Inner Traditions, Rochester VT.

Shakespeare, William

    1961 *Antony and Cleopatra*, ed. Louis Wright and Virginia LaMar. Washington Square Press, New York.

Smith, Anne

    2011 *The Performance of 16th-Century Music: Learning from the Theorists*. Oxford University Press, Oxford UK.

Solis, Marcelo

    n.d. *The History of Tango*. https://escuelatangoba.com/marcelosolis/category/history-of-tango/.

Solms, Mark

    1999 The Interpretation of Dreams and the Neurosciences. In *Freud's Tramdeutung*. Fischer Verlag, Frankfurt am Main DE.

Sorrenti, Carmen

    2018 *Pholarchos Tarot*, First Edition. Arnell Art, https://www.aando@arnellart.com.

    2022 The Pholarcos Tarot: A Pack of Alchemical Companions. https://www.carmensorrenti.com/services-nueva.

    2023 Personal communication, 2/4/2023.

Squarespace

    n.d. https://www.squarespace.com/.

Stanska, Suzanna

> 2022   The Mystery of the Mantegna Tarocchi. *DailyArt Magazine*. https://www.dailyartmagazine.com/mystery-mantegna-tarocchi/.

Switch-Sound File Converter

> n.d. https://www.nch.com.au/switch/index.html ?ns=true&kw=switch%20sound% 20file%20converter&gclid=EAIaIQobChMI6_SFucDCQIVBjBx0j5gBgEAAYASAAE gL8GfD_BwE.

Taylor, Thomas

> 2018 *Iamblichus on the Mysteries of the Egyptians, Chaldeans, and Assyrians*. Forgotten Books, London UK.

Temperance, Elani

> 2023   http://bearingtheaegis.blogspot.com/2017/10/the-doves-of-aphrodite.html.

Tennyson, Lord Alfred

> 2004 *Idylls of the King*. Dover Publications, New York.

Thompson, R. Campbell

> 1928 *The Gilgamesh Epic*. Luzac and Co., London, UK.

Van deCastle, Robert

> 1995 *Our Dreaming Mind*. Ballantine Books, New York.

Velikovsky, Immanuel

> 1950 *Worlds in Collision*.   Macmillan, New York.

Wagner, Richard

> n.d. *Tristan und Isolde*. https://www.youtube.com/watch?v=IdjFBW-S3z0.

Waite, Arthur E.

> 1991 *The Rider Tarot Deck*. U.S. Games Systems, Stamford CT.

Wigington, Patti

> 2018   A Brief History of Tarot. https://www.learnreligions.com/a-brief-history-of-tarot-2562770.

Wilhelm, Helmut

> 1967 *The I Ching, or Book of Changes*. Trans. Cary F. Baynes. *Bollingen Series* XIX. Princeton University Press, Princeton NJ.

About the Author

Dr. Curtiss Hoffman is professor emeritus of Anthropology at Bridgewater State University in Massachusetts. He is the author of *The Seven Story Tower: A Mythic Journey through Space and Time,* and *Stone Prayers: Native American Stone Constructions of the Eastern Seaboard,* as well as numerous articles and book chapters on dreams, myth, and archaeology. He is an amateur dulcianist and is a leading member of the International Association for the Study of Dreams.

www.ingramcontent.com/pod-product-compliance
Lightning Source LLC
Chambersburg PA
CBHW061117170426
43199CB00026B/2951